WHAT'S FOR YOU IS FOR YOU

What's For You Is For You!

Published by Krystal Lee Enterprises (KLE Publishing)
Copyright © 2020 by K. Lee All rights reserved.

Please send comments and questions:

Krystal Lee Enterprises
KrystalLeeEnterprises.com
KLEpub.com
sales@klepub.com
www.KLEPub.com   770-240-0089 Ext. 1

Author K Lee:
Social: @authorklee
Website: AuthorKLee.com

Email: me@authorklee.com

Printed in the United States of America.

All rights reserved. No part of this book may be reproduced or transmitted in any form or by any means, electronic or mechanical, including photocopying, recording or any information storage and retrieval system without written permission of the publisher except for brief quotations used in reviews, written specifically for inclusion in a newspaper, blog, magazine, or academic paper.

ISBN: 978-1-945066-06-1

Prop & Wardrobe Suggested List

2 Leaf Fans
5 Breast Plate for Guards and Cup Bearer
1 Coat of Many Colors
1 Table
13 Chairs
Khaki pants/shorts & White T Shirts for Hebrews
1 Chase Chair
1 Gold Rug
3 Cots
3 Thin sheets
Egyptian Men: White Shorts and Shirt
1 Fancy Chair
3 Tea Cup
1 Tea Pot
Head gear for Egyptians
12 sashes in different solid colors for each brother
3 Ropes of different lengths
1 Gold Crown & Specter
1 Silver Crown & Specter or a smaller Gold one
1 Large fake tree
1 Small Plant or Fake tree
Farming tools
1 Wagon
White Dresses for Egyptian Women
Children Wear All white
Pharaoh Gold shirt, white shorts, Gold Sash
Khaki skirts and white shirts Hebrew women for extras
All men wear khaki bottoms and white shirt

What's for You is for YOU!

A Stage Play by K. Lee Produced by Krystal Lee Enterprises

Bible Reference: Genesis 37 – 50, Apocrypha Books: Jasher, 12 Patriarchs. Character List & Actors: All Characters are adults except for youth theater.

1. Gad: _____
2. Cup Bearer: _____
3. Asher: _____
4. Baker: _____
5. Dan: _____
6. Potiphar: _____
7. Ruben: _____
8. Judah: _____
9. Joseph: _____
10. Benjamin: _____
11. Israel: _____
12. Pharaoh: _____
13. Midianite: _____
14. Potiphar's Wife: _____
15. Egyptian Lady 1: _____
16. Egyptian Lady 2: _____
17. Joseph's Wife: _____
18. Manasseh: _____
19. Ephraim: _____
20. Simeon: _____
21. Zebulun: _____
22. Naphtali: _____
23. Levi: _____

24. Issachar: _____
25. Guard (2): _____
26. Royal Guards (4): _____
27. Fan (2): _____
28. Prison Guard: _____
29. Ishmaelite (3): _____
30. Narrator: _____
31. Servant Girl: _____

Other Characters for Videos, Performances, & Transitions: (Optional)

32. Rachel: _____
33. Leah: _____
34. Abraham: _____
35. Lot: _____
36. Sarah: _____
37. Ishmael: _____
38. Isaac: _____
39. Jacob: _____
40. Esau: _____
41. Rebecca: _____
42. Cain: _____
43. Abel: _____
44. Mime Dancer (2): _____
45. Dancers (3): _____
46. Singer: _____
47. Poet: _____
48. Choir: _____
49. Comedian: _____
50. Drummer: _____

CONTENTS

ACT ONE: 7

ACT TWO: 69

ACT THREE: 125

AUTHOR: 171

Act One

Scene One

FADE UP FROM BLACK. CURTAIN IS PULLED SHUT.

NARRATOR: In the land of Canaan, there lived a Hebrew family. Born of Abraham, Isaac, and Jacob who the Lord named Israel. This nation was selected by Yahweh, appointed to be His people, and to live for His glory. Like us today they too had sibling rivalries, family issues, and gifts that could spread jealousy.

Having the Lord's favor in your life or in one's family doesn't negate the possibility that sin and the works of the enemy may come upon you. But it demonstrates that no matter the test, the trial, or problems the Lord is there with you to help you grow and become the perfect work He started in you.

CURTAINS ARE DRAWN BACK. Joseph, Asher, Gad, and Dan are present. Joseph is working to tend the sheep while his brothers sit upon the ground.

NARRATOR: Now, Joseph and his brothers Asher, Gad, and Dan are on the countryside of a land called Canaan. This sheep herding family comes from a family of shepherds. This family's name is well known in the land. They are the descendants of Abraham, Isaac, and Jacob who became Israel. This day the men were sent to shepherd the flock together. Joseph is up working while his brothers sit upon the ground watching him struggle. He is not used to working in the field like his older brothers and it shows.

JOSEPH: You guys need to get up and help me.

ASHER: Who made him the boss?

DAN: What are we supposed to be doing again?

GAD: Tending the flock didn't you know?

ASHER: So the young grasshopper is ready to rule?

JOSEPH: I'm just out here because Dad sent me. It's not fair I'm out here doing the work that we all should be doing. Plus, I'm missing out on my studies to babysit.

ASHER: Babysit?

GAD: Last time I checked we were all older than you. So you're just earning your keep.

DAN: Y'all did hear that, because Dad sent me out here. I'm surprise this little dude didn't say my daddy.

JOSEPH: Look, you guys say what you want. But I'm not going home to tell dad I did nothing all day. Y'all can be your own disappointment.

ASHER: Okay, we have heart today. Careful guys, you know we have a tattle-tail with us.

JOSEPH: We all know how this goes. We go home, and dad's gonna ask me a question about y'all. I tell the truth. I can't lie to him and y'all know it. Y'all get in trouble because you choose to. You probably hate me for stuff that's not my fault. If you know what he said, why not get it done so we all can just go home?

ASHER: So everything you're asked to do you do? Aren't you the perfect son?

JOSEPH: I'm not trying to be special.

ASHER, GAD, DAN: But we all know you ARE!

JOSEPH: Look y'all want to know what we talk about during our studies? I don't have any secrets.

GAD: We got a good idea.

JOSEPH: So that's a no?

DAN: I want to know? What y'all talk about?

JOSEPH: Dad tells me about Abraham. How our grandfather was promised to have seed the number of the sand. How everything in his sight would be his. This promise was made to him by God. So I believe it's going to happen.

Video Play Back: Voice over. Image of Abraham standing looking at a desert land.

Voice of God/Narrator: God will surely bless Abraham, and that his offspring will be multiplied as numerous as the stars in the sky and the sand on the seashore. Furthermore, his offspring will possess the gate of his enemies.

ASHER: Wait, so you spend those lessons talking about your inheritance?

JOSEPH: Don't you get it. Abraham and Lot increased together and when their wealth couldn't thrive together they separated.

(Optional) Play Video Flashback of Abraham and Lot or Live performance.

ABRAHAM: NEPHEW, look at how good God has become. We are thriving in the land. It is hard to believe that I was once a wanted man by King Nimrod, but I am still here. I should be dead so many times over, but God!

LOT: Yes, Uncle. All of this is a blessing, but if I am honest, I came to speak with you because there is also a problem.

ABRAHAM: Tell me what it is nephew, and we can sort the problem now.

LOT: It's not a battle, but more of a domestic problem. You see, you , your people, servants, and cattle have increased substantially and so has mine. We could easily be neighbors, but now, the water is getting scarce and so is the land. Our animals are grazing in the same places, so we are losing the battle for being able to live so closely together.

ABRAHAM: I see. I would have loved to live

around you all of my days, but I understand that when Yah moves, He can give us more than we even ask for, right?

Lot nods his head in agreement.

ABRAHAM: Then tell me, what part of the land would you like to take?

LOT: If it is alright with you Uncle, I would like to take the land here.

NARRATOR: The land Lot picked was flowing with milk and honey. It had streams, trees, and pretty scenic views to die for. He had a set up that would be seen as a gift from God for anybody. He was blessed if Abraham said "yes." Not to mention, the only reason Lot has as much as he does, is because Abraham helped him get it all. It could be argued that Abraham should haven gotten the better of the land because of his efforts.

ABRAHAM: I trust that Yahweh laid it on your heart for what land to choose, and it will be as you say. You can have it. I will take the other lands and see what our God has for me. What's for me Is For Me, and What's for You, is For You.

Optional: Video payback of items appearing as presented in the text of Joseph.

JOSEPH: Abraham had confidence in what was for him will be for him and he allowed Lot to choose first. Lot chose the Land that best appeared to flow with milk and honey. The land was alive with streams, trees, vegetation, and life. Abraham took the latter. The land that was a desert. It seemed dead, or at least required a lot of work to appear the way the land Lot picked. But with Yah, The almighty Elohim, He took what Abraham saw and gave it to him as his inheritance. Said everything he could see would be his. He made the land give milk, honey, beauty and brought life where there was death. He gave him as many sons as the grains of sand beneath his feet! Don't you see the poetry in this? The Creator, was not intimidated nor afraid to give a dry land life.

POET: Poem on bringing life where there was none. This can be an original poem or use the inserted poem. Drummer plays with poet. There can also be dancers.

With success so great, can you imagine your plate appearing empty, or your blessing coming late?
You are a marvel, a man with a golden fist, ev-

erything you touch turns to gold,
You're not perfect, but your life and wealth is legendary,
You trusted Yah when it mattered, you leaned on God when everyone needed to know,
You are the father of many nations because you proved to be faithful,
You allowed God Almighty to bless you, keep you, and tell you His vision for your story.
You never robbed Yah of His glory,
So he increased you, and you blessed Melchizedek with a seed after inheriting the largest desert,
In what could seem like lost, You demonstrated how God was still boss!
The example of not perfection, but of divine protection,
Yah choose you to bring His nation through, to show the world His goodness and man,
How what is for you, is truly for you!
That's the end of this dance...

DAN: So what you saying?

JOSEPH: Okay, let me put it in a language that might be closer to your heart. Still on Abraham. You remember Sarah, our grandmother. (They agree). She was married and that meant she belonged to Abraham as his inheritance and prized possession. But when Abraham had to go around kings, he thought to lie and say they were relatives then husband and wife. The two kings who tried to bewife Sarah both brought plagues and afflictions on themselves because Sarah belonged to Abraham. What was for him, was for him. No man or king could change that.

ASHER: All that is nice, you have always been crafty with words. But tell us the truth. What do y'all really talk about?

JOSEPH: Look you guys are all older than me if anyone should feel left out it's me or Benjamin. If I'm not worried about my inheritance why should any of you?

DAN: Wait do you really believe the special son won't have an inheritance? I wouldn't be surprised if we are left with nothing. After all, my mother is Bilhah.

GAD: Our mom is Zipah, nobody cares about servant children. Do you recall the account of Ishmael and Isaac? Ishmael was shafted. He wasn't the child of promise, he was simply blessed and sent on his way.

Optional: Flashback Video or live performance. Dancers can transition the stage.

SARAH: Abraham, I love Ishmael, but he has to go. You know things will get more complicated for the both of them as they get older. We have to take the bandaid off.

ABRAHAM: This is painful for me Sarah, I love both of my sons, but I do know the will of Yah will be established.

SARAH: He promised us a son, and I can only apologize for my part in this, but I will not allow Hagar to profit any more from my mistakes.

ABRAHAM: I understand. I will be the one to send them away. Please let me say a proper goodbye to my son.

SARAH: Of course, I trust you. Do what you feel is best. But for Hagar, I will dismiss her for you. I will send in Ishmael.

Abraham agrees. His first born son enters the room moments later.

ABRAHAM: Son, it is good to see you. I have news for you.

ISHMAEL: Have I disappointed you father?

ABRAHAM: No. I want to speak to you about a journey you will take with your mother, and how I need you to go trusting God like I told you. I need you to understand that this goodbye is not forever, but it is see you soon.

ISHMAEL: I figured something like this would happen considering the tension in the house. My mom said I would get sent away. I get it dad, but I cannot say that I am happy about it.

ABRAHAM: You are a man now, 19 years old, I got the chance to see you grow into a man and I inparted in you, what has kept me over the years. My God will not leave nor forsake you, but give you what is yours. All will be well, and I will see you soon. You are not leaving empty handed for I will always be with you. You are my son, but your mother is struggling, and we both know it.

ISHMAEL: Yeah, she is. I get it. As long as you promise to visit, I can move in my life's direction. Don't abandon me dad.

ABRAHAM: Never. You will always be part of my home.

The two men embrace.

JOSEPH: To be fair. Ishmael was given a promise as well as his mother to always have. If you read the book of Jasher you too will find, Abraham never stopped pursuing him in fact he helped him weed out the bad wife for the best wife. Then, after some years, he moved closer to his Father's home. Did you also know that when Isaac was to be sacrificed before Elohim, Ishmael went with them?

JOSEPH: He didn't go to the rock but he walked miles to support both Isaac and Abraham. He wasn't allowed to come to the site of the sacrifice as the Lord didn't permit it. What was in store for Isaac, and the command to Abraham, they couldn't change. The Lord doesn't promise to be fair, but He is just. What was intended for each of them, they did have. So as you see, Ishmael wasn't left behind, he just got what the Good Lord intended. Stop allowing yourself to see things so one sided.

ASHER: Your special because you were born of the only woman dad wanted. It's no secret. Leah may have been her twin, but I'm not sure if it was the eyes or what, but your mother had his heart.

DAN: Our mothers were more or less property. Not sure what that makes us?

JOSEPH: Why are you guys talking like this? I can't change who my mother is—was. You would think her dying would make us all closer. Bilhah, your mother has been so kind and you know I love them all like family, because we are! Dad loving my mom had nothing to do with me or any of us! We can't make there problems ours. We are brothers.

GAD: But I am sure you enjoy the benefits.

JOSEPH: I didn't ask for this. Last time I checked Dad had to be friendly with all of our mothers or we wouldn't be here. Check Bilhah's bed chamber (or house) and you will see who dad loves and spends his time with. You should be slow to speak.

DAN: Watch your mouth!

JOSEPH: Are you guys really not going to help me?

ASHER: That's his serious voice guys, I think we better get up.

GAD: Or is it his tattle-tail voice, hard to tell?

JOSEPH: That's it, I'm gone. Don't know why dad sends me out here anyway.

DAN: Run off like you always do. We're trying to help you become a man. Your daddy can't save you forever!

Joseph exits stage left.

ASHER: I can't stand that kid.

GAD: Hey you don't choose your family.

DAN: But we could. We didn't choose the lives we have, but we can choose the future we create.

GAD: You're talking stupid.

ASHER: What's your point Dan?

DAN: I'm just saying, one day after tending the sheep, we could just ensure he doesn't come back.

GAD: What you talking about Dan?

DAN: You know what I'm saying.

ASHER: Gad you want an inheritance don't you? What chance do we have competing with Joseph, Benjamin, Ruben, or Judah and the rest of them? Rachael and Leah's kids will get everything. Dan you have another brother to think about too. The kid said, what's for us is for us.

DAN: You mean what's for you is for you.

GAD: Kill that. If we take what's for us, there won't be nothing.

ASHER: Life is not about sitting back letting life happen, it's about taken what's yours. The young kid got all these stories. But let me tell you about a story he didn't share. There were two sons born together, twins. One came out and the second holding his heel.

GAD: Right. They grew up together. One was strong and the other smart. The one that was strong slayed King Nimrod and a guard, the other stayed at home kissing up to momma. The mom played favorites like women tend to do.

Optional: Video Flashback or live performance.

NARRATOR: Rebecca was pregnant, and reminiscing on a prophecy she heard. She knew her second son would be greater than the older, and would be born holding his heel.

REBECCA is sitting at the table when Jacob comes in and sits.

JACOB: Mom, tell me you have some good news for me?

REBECCA: Your father's condition is worsening in his eyes. I am not sure how long he will be able to see.

JACOB: Do you think, I could do something to get him to see that I am the right son to bless?

REBECCA: Your dad is stubborn, but he listens to God. He won't argue but he feels that Esau is like him and should get the birthright as customary.

JACOB: So then, that is it for me, Mom. I cannot beat Esau at anything. I am not a better hunter, stronger, or even have a larger beard. He has red hair and I have black hair. He is better than me in every way.

REBECCA: But Jacob, these are not the things that Yah pays attention to. I know what I heard, and I know that our God doesn't lie. What's for You is For You, and this is for you son. Let me help you.

JACOB: How can you do that?

REBECCA: If we cannot convince your father that you are the son to bless, maybe we need to convince him that you are the son he should bless.

JACOB: I don't follow.

REBECCA: You just listen to me and Momma will take care of this. I am going to need a baby goat, but I need you to make a skin of fur that feels like your brother's hair. You work on getting me what I need, and I will cook a meal fit for you to be king!

ASHER: The one who went out and killed King Nimrod to avenge his grandfather, i.e Abraham our great-grandfather, knew his head was required so he sold his birth right for some food. But this trickster after taken the birth right was not finished. He wanted the blessing too. So the mom and he tricked the Father, Isaac our grandfather, who was half blind into blessing the trickster instead of the eldest.

As Jacob kneeled at the bedside of a restless ISSAC who was full from the yummy food, he spoke.

ISSAC: Esau, that was excellent game. If I didn't know better, I would have said your mother cooked it and put her foot in it.

Jacob didn't speak but sat there listening.

ISSAC: I am not sure if my hearing is going to. I cannot hear you say a peep. Come closer and let me touch you son. I cannot see your face, but I want to bless you.

Jacob came closer and made sure to keep the animal fur closest to his father. He kept kneeling down so his dad did not feel any other part of his body.

ISSAC: My good son, who I am very well pleased with. Thank you for blessing me and becoming great in everything you do. You will make our nation proud with your hunting and skills to lead. You have been a fighter since birth, pulling your brother and our family. Now, it is time for me to give you what only I can, my blessing.

ISSAC: Father, may you smile upon my son today. May you be well pleased with him, and show him the favor that you showed my father, Abraham. May you give him, what you promised our family. May he be a good representation of you for the nations. May he never lack, struggle, or suffer--and should that be the case, may you turn it always for his good.

ISSAC: Thank you Father for smiling down on him and given me the strength to pass on my blessing before I close my eyes for the last time. In the name of Yahowah, Yahweh, the God who is in the breath, our inhale and exhale, we say thank you. Shalom, peace and blessings to you.

As Issac was about to embrace Jacob for the last time, in walks Esau with his bowl.

ESAU: Father, I have prepared a prized kill for you today that you will certainly love.

He walks in and sees Jacob lowered before their father and he is angry.

ESAU: What are you doing here Jacob?

ISSAC: Jacob? Is this you?

JACOB: It is me father.

ISSAC: Why have you done this to me?

ESAU: Why have you done this to us? Are you

this greedy Jacob? I sold you my birthright because you and mom tricked me, but now, you trick Dad for the blessing? You are a monster!

JACOB: I didn't make you sell your birthright, you gave it up. I am to blame for this, but this belongs to me and I wasn't alone. It's all part of God's plan.

ISSAC: If this is Yah's plan, why does it feel so wrong? You should have trusted Him like the rest of us to give you what He has for you. Now, you will have suffering and correction.

JACOB: I'm sorry dad, you're right. I just couldn't be wrong about this.

ISSAC: You will learn like Abraham and Sarah, what it costs to sidestep God's plan. What's for you is yours Son, you don't have to steal, lie, or cheat to get it. Now, go and pray for forgiveness and mercy. That's all you can do now.

Jacob leaves. Esau comes closer to Issac.

ESAU: Dad, what do I do? Can you bless me now?

ISSAC: I gave it all to Jacob. I don't have a blessing for you. But I can pray the Father's will over your life, and that will be enough.

Esau kneeled down by the foot of his father.

GAD: And what was left for ESAU? Nothing but scraps that our grandfather, Isaac, could think up to bless him because our beloved Father, Jacob, tricked him out of everything. He took it all.

ASHER: Do you want to be ESAU? Begging for remnants? Or do you want to be Jacob, Israel, your father and all of our father, who took everything for himself?

DAN: I want what is for me. But y'all joking about you know murder, right?

PAUSE

ASHER: Yeah, of course.

DAN: I'm sure dad is thinking of us all. Plus, you know the story of Cain and Abel. After Cain killed Abel, his blood cried out for vengeance to the Lord and the earth spat him up twice.

Optional: Video Flashback or live performance.

Abel is speaking to Cain.

ABEL: Aren't you a little bit excited for today?

CAIN: To slaughter a perfectly fit lamb? Naw, I'm good.

ABEL: You are looking at this all wrong. This is the day we get to give our first fruits to Yahweh. You know how long I've wanted to do this? Our parents have carried us all of our lives, but now we get to build a relationship with Him for ourselves.

CAIN: Yeah, all that sounds great. I will have something to bring Him that will be good.

ABEL: I pray you are not giving him that sick lamb tied up to the post outside. His eyes look cross-sided, and he walks with a limp, Cain.

CAIN: Mind your business. It might be a runt, but it is perfectly healthy. All creatures were made by God, so I am sure He will love it.

ABEL: Don't you know that withholding from God only means withholding from yourself? The One who brought you here and every animal on this planet, is asking you for one perfect lamb, and you won't do it?

CAIN: How do you know He cares so much? You are only bringing grains or something. You don't know everything. We have been on earth about the same amount of time, so chill.

ABEL: Suit yourself! What's for You is For You, for the good or the bad. I won't the good! I'm out.

Abel leaves.

DAN: You know what it took for Cain to get right with God? He couldn't, he tried to pay the price and he ended up dying, depending on the account you read, by arrow by his great nephew, or a house falling on him when he fled home after being hit. Either version seems pretty painful. He never could live among his family and had to live in the valley while they lived in the cliff of the rock. I don't think we won't that. Do you want to give up everything for taking an innocent life?

ASHER: He's not all that innocent if you ask me. Abel, was cool, but he isn't the little cocky, know-it-all brother we have. He needs to be knocked down a few steps, that's all.

DAN: Trust me, we all know that is true. But, we will be alright.

GAD: Well, let's get up and do something. We're going to hear Dad's mouth, but less if we finish.

Scene Two

Inside the living space, there is a long table, 13 chairs. Israel is working on the coat of many colors as Joseph walks in. Joseph comes in but he is looking away from Israel, looking back as if he has lost something and pacing in a circle. Israel puts the coat down on the closest chair to him and sits closer to watch as Joseph paces the room.

JOSEPH: Dad, I'm tired of this!

ISRAEL: Calm down son, what's wrong?

JOSEPH: I swear they hate me.

ISRAEL: No need swearing and caring on. Tell me what happened.

JOSEPH: They don't listen to you. I told them what you said. They just sat around most of the day and they did nothing.

ISRAEL: I'll talk with them when they come in later… (Joseph motions to say he's not done.)

There's more, come on, talk to me.

JOSEPH: There is no point in us working together. I am better off here with you or alone if I have to do things by myself.

ISRAEL: Joseph you and your brothers have to learn how to love each other. Someday, I will not be here, same as my father, he had to move on. Always be focused on looking and moving forward. Don't think for a second you don't need your brothers. You're all brothers for a reason and you all have gifts, talents that make you stronger together. What's your gift is yours, but don't think your gift outweighs anyone else's. You are a dreamer, gifted scholar, but a dream is a dream, and knowledge information if you don't have doers. People you can lead and want to share your dreams with.

ISRAEL: We're good now?

JOSEPH: I think—No I know they hate me because they think you love me more than them.

ISRAEL: I see. Does this have something to do with their inheritance?

JOESPH: They brought it up.

ISRAEL: Don't worry. The Lord has enough for us all. Don't let them trouble you about what you will have, and what they think they won't. Talk like this gets man to stop focusing on what's for them in exchange for what's for someone else. Abraham, Seth, Enoch got promises only meant for them. Can we fall under the promise? Yes, but that promise was made to them for them. We have the account, we don't say story because it's truth, to encourage us for the unique things The Almighty will do for us, for you. There will only be one Joseph.

JOSEPH: Right…except for the millions of other men born in the future called Joseph.

ISRAEL: Yes, of course, there is that, but the accounts of our forefathers demonstrates the Lord's ability, character, and power. He is never tapped out of resources nor promises. When we attempt to box the Creator, we put limits and our thoughts, ways, before His. He's called a creator because He creates. But we try and put limits on Yahweh, the only true and living God, and make our thoughts and ways greater than His.

ISRAEL: Your brothers haven't learned to trust Yahweh to be their promise maker; but if they think they can take what's yours, they are mistaken. They can't take it but only walk away from what is theirs. Don't ever let anyone take from you what is yours and give what is due to whom it belongs because that is their lot in life. The Lord has plans for you and all of us, you remember that.

JOSEPH: But dad you don't hear them like I do. They think Benjamin and Aunt Leah's sons or I will take everything.

ISRAEL: It's a long story that can be made short by saying this. The choices we make in life, the good and the bad, will give us a harvest. Remember you reap what you sow. As a young man, I had plans, thoughts that I believed were just. I thought by changing the playing field I could ensure my lot in life being the younger brother to Esau. But my foolish and selfish choices cost me.

ISRAEL: What I bought for a bowl of food was mine. But what I took by deceiving my father, I didn't have enough money or time to pay for it. I am still paying for that mistake but because of Elohim's grace, He is sufficient to walk me through. Deliverance is not always in an obstacle being removed, sometimes it's in going through the fire that purifies you. It changes your thinking, refreshes your soul, perception,--and yes brings you to repentance. I tricked my father and in the end I got tricked, too. But I learned from that. Have faith in Yah to be the greatest teacher.

JOSEPH: I didn't trick my brothers. I haven't wronged them—with all due respect. I'm just trying to help them.

Optional: Video Element - Rachel taking the figure and putting it in her bag. Then Israel finding it amongst her things. Then, Israel hugging and mourning the lost of Rachel but her trying to keep him positive. She is apologetic.

ISRAEL: Hear me again. Your mom, Rachel I loved. I worked for her for 7 years only to find out I had to work 7 more to keep her. And when I ran, she took idols from her father without me knowing. My father-in-law told my brother I stole them and he believed him. He thought once a trickster always a trickster. My father in law then sought me out and found me, and demanded his idols back. I told him I didn't have them but I will find them and whoever took them will die.

ISRAEL: So I searched and a familiar voice, loving voice told me she had them. I wanted to ask why, but that didn't matter. What was done was done. The Lord granted His promise of two sons, then she died giving birth to Benjamin. I loved your mother, and a child born of love will always be prized over those born of obligation. I know you are too young to understand this, but trust me, when you find love, nothing will make you more pleased than to marry that woman and have children of your own.

JOSEPH: I hear you, but are you saying you only loved mom?

ISRAEL: I'm saying I love all my sons, my children, because I know they are a gift from the Father of Life. You are all unique, sent with your own gifts. I love you differently because you are all different. To love you all the same would be unfair. You are not a fast runner, but Naphtali is and I love that about him. Judah is incredibly strong, I can't say much for your small arms, but I love that about Judah. You see what I am saying? Yes, I love you all, and I love you each more for your differences. Now, that's enough of that for today. Look, I want to show you something.

Israel and Joseph walk over to a chair where they gaze upon a new garment full of colors.

JOSEPH: Wow, this is nice, I've never seeing anything like it. Who made it?

ISRAEL: Of course I did.

JOSEPH: Nobody can say a man can't sew (they shake on it. Then he further inspects it.) I see the skills, this coat must of cost some serious money, and time. The material. So where are you going to wear it to?

ISRAEL: I'm not wearing it, you are.

JOSEPH: Wait you saying this is for me?

ISRAEL: You were on my mind and I wanted to give you something to let you know how much you mean to me.

JOSEPH: All I can say is thanks, Dad! This is wow, thanks.

ISRAEL: I'm glad you like it. Gone and put it on and tell your brothers I said come to me when there done.

JOSEPH: How do you know they even got up from the ground?

ISRAEL: I know all of my sons. Just go tell

them.

Joseph exits stage.

NARRATOR: Parents are to train up a child in the way they should go. Praying over your children is a must; knowing their gifts and talents helps parents to pray for what their children need. This is the caring love all children need.

Spotlight on Israel.

ISRAEL: Lord what a fine man he will turn out to be. I pray him and his brothers strengthen their bond and understand, they are brothers no matter their mother. I—you are their Father. Keep them close Elohim and show them what you have for them, assure them that what is for them will be. I am not a perfect man, and perhaps not a perfect father. Forgive me and my heart if I am in error, and help me to share my genuine love for all my sons. You have gifted each of them, and I love what I see about them. I understand different children require love to be shown in different ways. Lord help me to do a better job.

Lights Fade.

Scene Three

NARRATOR: Back in the fields, the brothers are busy working. The brothers are moving some hay around and Asher stops working to sit when he saw Joseph coming. He starts smiling and sits down on top of a bundle of hay. Joseph planned to see the guys far up on the hill and let them know their father is waiting for them at home. He doesn't hesitate to show off his new robe to his brothers and they all take notice.

JOSEPH: Hey, Dad told me to tell you to finish your work and head back to the house. He wants to talk to y'all.

ASHER: What a nice robe you have Joseph.

JOSEPH: Yeah, thanks.

Up looks Dan and Gad from working.

DAN: Who gave that to you I didn't see that in your closet? We know it wasn't your mother's.

GAD: Hey that was low, Rachel was cool and respect the dead. But I agree, where you get the coat?

JOSEPH: Dad made it for me.

DAN: Made it for you?

JOSEPH: Yeah, you know like got the fabric, sewed it together, picked it all himself.

ASHER: Why don't you get out of here. Go home. We got the message. Plus, I am sure your sweating like a stripper in church with that coat on. It's hot out here.

Joseph exits.

ASHER: Y'all still think we're going to have an inheritance with dad spending a fortune on fabric? Who is this guy? Gucci, Prada, or maybe he thinks he is Guess? I guess.

ASHER: You know we ain't heard about none of them people. But maybe y'all have?

DAN: The time it took him to make that, he could have came out here and tilled the grounds himself! He acting like his life is so busy, but he has enough time to make a coat of many colors? Who does that?

GAD: If y'all had money, y'all would spend it how you wanted to. But I know he better not be the only one to get a coat. I mean, I'm at least better than you two.

ASHER: Yeah, whatever. You expecting your coat when you get home? Right. All I'm saying is we need dad to hold on to it long enough for us to have something. There ain't gone be no coat for none of us when we get home and you know that. He probably feeds us only so we can work.

DAN: Man you ain't never lied.

GAD: I ain't hearing y'all. I'm Special. "This Little light of mine, I'm gonna let it shine. Everywhere I go, I'm gonna let it shine. Let it shine, let it shine." Yeah, I can't speak for y'all but my daddy loves me. Daddy, loves me, ohh yes he does, for the—

ASHER: Please stop.

GAD: You can best believe I got a key chain, scarf, a pair of socks or something.

DAN: Don't count on that, and with that voice, don't expect a music contract, or to ever sing solo at church. Just Terrible.

ASHER: Man, Rachel got a lick beating with-Leah. Leah didn't know what she had, but we ain't making her same mistake. At least, I ain't.

DAN: Why I get the feeling we bout to head down memory lane?

GAD: What other street we gone be on to talk about the Past?

Optional: Flashback Video Scene.

ASHER: Just be quiet so maybe you two can learn something. And our ears hear something pleasant after that. Yo, for real, though. The bet of the century is when Rachel asked Leah for help to get pregnant. Rachel traded time with dad, so that she could have two children. If she wouldn't have come to Leah, the two children she had, would have also been born by Leah. But Rachel had something Leah wanted. She wanted to be desired like any mother would by her husband. She wanted what Rachel had so badly, that she gave a blessing to Rachel to have children. I guess they both wanted what the other had. Read about it in Jasher. This is why he is here. He should have been just like us. He's not so special.

Optional: Continued Video Element - Leah and Rachel talking about children. Leah gives her two acorn looking objects as they negotiate sitting at a table. The montage shows Rachel getting pregnant twice. Then ultimately, her demise.

ASHER: We're done. Let's get out of here and meet our maker.

DAN: Why you make it sound like death.

ASHER: I can think of one thing that needs to die around here.

They are all walking off stage. Gad stops and turns to Asher.

GAD: What you talking about Asher? Some good goat? I can go for some bagging curry right now.

DAN: No idiot, Favoritism.

ASHER: Huh, right, right, favoritism. Let's go have some goat. I was gonna say that.

Scene Four

Israel and Joseph are sitting together outside, and they are discussing a piece of artwork.

JOSEPH: Dad I just had a weird thought. I think my brothers are in trouble.

ISRAEL: Why do you say that Joseph?

JOSEPH: I see wolves, coming out of nowhere in droves for the sheep. Surrounding me to kill me, but it could be them. I think they may need our help. When I went to go and check on the sheep, a ram was dead. When I went to touch it, a wolf woke up and tried to attack me.

ISRAEL: You stay here. I will be right back. Sometimes our minds play tricks on us, sometimes it can be something. But I'll be right back.

Israel takes off with his staff up the path and the brothers hear his call out to them. They all come running up to him, Judah, Ruben and the others included.

GAD: I knew you would come for me. So dad where is my scarf? Socks? Tie? Shorts? Necklace?

ISRAEL: Boy I ain't got nothing for you, but I have a bone to pick with all of you.

ISRAEL: Sons you know when I send you out what I expect you to do. What happened today? Okay… so no one has anything to say? I heard you do a lot of talking when you out, then you get here and crickets. It's a shame I have to send your baby brother out to keep an eye on you and help; he's the baby. I am trusting for you all to train him up in the right way and he's telling me y'all can't do that and he is training you. Am I missing something? I also heard y'all worried about an inheritance, huh?

GAD: Dad we were just joking with him. No harm was intended.

ASHER: Trying to rough him up a bit.

DAN: You know he's too sensitive.

ISRAEL: I don't know what you guys are up to but I do know this. I have something for all my sons. That includes you, you, and you also the rest of you. But if I hear any more stupidness like this, you haven't seen work. And if you don't do it, the reason you won't have an inheritance will have nothing to do with Joseph, but everything to do with you. What's for you, is for you, and don't let yourself change that. Do I make myself clear?

The guys answer back, "of course Baba." They all start walking ahead towards the house. Israel calls for Judah and Ruben to stay back a second.

ISRAEL: Judah, Ruben, I expect more from the both of you. I don't know how the others may behave, but you two are my strong sons, the others look up to you. I need you both to look out for Joseph and do what we know to do, "take care of each other." Do you understand me?

Ruben and Judah: (Murmuring) "Yes sir."

ISRAEL: You getting quite again.

Ruben and Judah: (Louder) "Yes Sir."

ISRAEL: Alright.

They are all approaching the front of the house but don't enter just yet because Joseph comes running to meet them.

Enters Joseph.

JOSEPH: Dad I had a dream, you won't believe it; it was crazy.

ISRAEL: Well tell us what happened, we're done here?

JOSEPH: Right, so I took a nap after coming back like you said and this dream came to me while I slept. We were binding sheaves of grain out in the field when suddenly my sheaf rose and stood upright, while your sheaves gathered around mine and bowed down to it. Dad, what do you think that means?

ASHER: You think we are going to bow down to you Joseph? This must be a joke, are we getting Punk'd? We are not in the same timezone right now. Can't be! Somebody got a camera in the audience making a reel of this?

DAN: I'm stuck on the, you would reign over us part. Show me the cameras. Yo I agree, is this for the Gram, TikTok, Facebook live, Snapchat, or Youtube? This has to be a joke. (optional) Is Tiktok still a thing? Because it is here one day, gone the next. We don't know what's going on!

GAD: Like now. Is it me or am I overlooking where you secretly put my socks, scarf, or something somewhere for me to go an find right now? (He is searching around items outside) I like nice things. First you give him a coat, now his sheaf is larger than mine? Who does this kid think he is, the King of Egypt?

ISRAEL: Everyone hold your horses it's just a dream. No need to get worked up over a dream. Boys go wash up and get ready for dinner. Joseph you stay here.

The guys all enter the house, they all exit except Israel and Joseph.

JOSEPH: Dad what do you think it means?

ISRAEL: I have an idea of what it means. You have to be careful of how you speak your dreams in front of your brothers. I appreciate your dreams, but sometimes they may misunderstand them—you know?

JOSEPH: So you're saying you want me to keep them to myself?

ISRAEL: No I'm saying, tell me, and we'll see when the time is right to share with your brothers.

JOSEPH: Alright, for me to be the sensitive one, I can name a few that are more sensitive than me. Did you see Judah's face? I ain't trying to call anyone a hater, but Judah and Simeon would both give a run for first place to tear off one of my limbs.

ISRAEL: It will be a little while for dinner. Maybe you should stay outside, write out your dream. Talk to the Lord about it. You know it is Yah that gives the understanding of any dream; the interpretation belongs to Him especially if He gave you the dream. Stay out here and take advantage of the sun.

JOSEPH: Alright, I will come in for dinner after.

ISRAEL: Good job, Son. I knew you were special.

Israel enters the house. Joseph sits down on a stump and he begins to pray and look to heaven.

Optional: Video Element: Sheaves of Grain play on the screen bowing to a larger sheave.

JOSEPH: Yahweh, what did my dream mean? How am I supposed to know who to tell my dreams to and how? Seems like no matter what I try to do to get along with my brothers, there's a problem. Sometimes I wish I could just be to myself and be away from them for a while.

JOSEPH: Not forever, just like a break. Lord, I don't see how they are going to bow to me, or how I will rise up above them, when they are all older, bigger, maybe not smarter but everything else than me. Lord show me how to be obedient, patient, a great son to my father, and a better brother to my brothers. I do love them and I pray I can prove it when it matters most.

Joseph YAWNS and leans his head back on the tree. Folding his arms, he rested against the tree.

Scene Five

The sons and their dad are sitting at the table. Sitting at the dinner table. Israel, Asher, Gad, Dan, Ruben, Simeon, Issachar, Zebulun, Judah, and the other brothers sit around the table. Everyone except Joseph. They are ready to eat with their forks in their hand, many have done a prayer to themselves.

ISRAEL: I haven't seen Joseph come in yet. Have you all seen him in the room?

RUBEN: No, I'm the last.

ISRAEL: Ruben, you mind running to get your brother?

Ruben drops his fork, he just sat down and picked up his fork.

RUBEN: No sir, I don't mind. (As he walks away) I'm sure he's wrapped in his colorful blanky snoozing like a young ram.

ISRAEL: Did I hear you?

RUBEN: No sir.

ISRAEL: Don't forget about what we talked about. You boys are family. Joseph's young and he needs you all to help him. I know some times it may not be easy, but you all went through this phase, too. I remember when Asher you were born. My 8th son right after Gad. You were trying to find your spot and sometime later, much later. You found it.

Enters Ruben and Joseph. Joseph is still wearing his coat as he goes over to his father and whispers.

JOSEPH: Dad, I have something to tell you after dinner.

Joseph goes to his seat.

GAD: What's the whispering for? You know we can all hear you right? It's a play, everyone can hear you, Fashinisto!

JOSEPH: It's nothing. I just need to talk to Dad after. That's what I said for y'all to hear directly.

ASHER: Are we not worthy to hear the conversation, O' Great King?

DAN: Is it another dream?

JOSEPH: Yes, it is another dream, and perhaps now may not be a good time to share.

ISRAEL: Yes, we're eating. Let's enjoy dinner.

RUBEN: I'm sure his dream can't be any worst than the first. Please Joseph, share with us your vision. Is it about farm animals?

Some at the table start laughing but not too hard or loudly.

JOSEPH: Dad?

ISRAEL: Go ahead Joseph.

JOSEPH: Well it's actually about stars.

ASHER: Here we go.

DAN: You've been doing too much reading or looking at too many pictures and you need to come back to earth, where there is gravity.

ISRAEL: Stars are very important, I have tried to teach you all about how to read the stars. You can locate people, places, and so much by knowing how to read the stars. Did any of you know that?

GAD: I wonder why we don't know…. Perhaps we all could benefit from a little one on one time like Joseph?

ISRAEL: Smart alec, maybe we should all just listen to him? Go ahead Joseph.

JOSEPH: Thanks. So first, I did what you said, I prayed for the interpretation of the first dream. I fell asleep and I believe the second dream explains the first. This time when I slept, I saw the sun and moon and eleven stars bowing down to me. How is that? I mean first sheaves of grain and now stars, that's crazy right?

ISRAEL: Wait a minute, Son. What is this dream you had? Will your mothers and I and your brothers actually come and bow down to the ground before you? Do you think that is what this dream is implying to you?

JOSEPH: I don't know—for sure. But the Lord

above controls my dreams, right? If He allows it, and allowed me to see it, is that what it means? You said the interpretations belong to Him.

Asher drops his spoon and pulls away from the table. Dan and Gad soon follow suit.

ASHER: I'm full.

DAN: Me too!

GAD: I'm just leaving.

RUBEN: I just got here so I'm going to finish my meal then I'm gone.

Scene Six

All the guys are in their space except Judah and Ruben. Some sitting others standing.

GAD: Okay I'm down.

DAN: Down for what?

ASHER: Controlling who stays in our family. That kid is a loose cannon. He's crazy to think he would rule over all of us.

DAN: And to bow down to him, dad and all our mothers, is crazy cocky. He is beyond help now. This is starting to feel real personal.

GAD: I didn't get a pair of socks? I mean what is happening to this family? Dad knows I got to keep my profile rocking. How am I supposed to do that with a social inept brother has more style than I do at the moment?

Ruben enters.

DAN: It's just Ruben.

RUBEN: What's up?

ASHER: Look we know you hate Joseph just as much as we do. You are the first born and if anyone should be entitled to us bowing down to them, it should be you. You're the oldest. Yet the dreamer said even you will bow.

RUBEN: I heard that. So what do we do about that? Can't stop the kid from dreaming.

In walks Judah. Everyone goes quiet.

JUDAH: What's going on? Why is everyone staring at me like I have a spot light on me and am about to do a solo? But I'm ready. (He starts singing a tune he knows, terribly).

SIMEON: Nah man, stop it. This is not a musical or we would all be fired. We were just talking.

JUDAH: Yeah, about what?

SIMEON: About our problem.

JUDAH: Can you be more specific?

DAN: We were going to discuss how we can eliminate the star child.

RUBEN: Wait a minute are you talking about killing Joseph?

ASHER: Well yeah, as long as he lives we are all fighting for scraps. Judah and Ruben you're both included. Think about it Simeon, Levi? You both took a whole city to avenge our sister. Did Joseph take such a risk? Has he lead any worthwhile battle for us? Or is he just a wimpy kid with a dad that is starry eyed for him?

GAD: Did you see the coat? I didn't get a coat, socks, handkerchief, hat, or a scarf. I like fashion.

DAN: Bro we know! He was actually looking forward to it. Think about it. What are you really hoping for? How are you going to get it, if Joseph steals the spotlight from all of us? What have you both if you bow down to Joseph? That is a reproach to your seniority, and an insult Judah to your size.

RUBEN: Killing him I think is too much, but we can pretend his dead. It's just as good as the real thing.

DAN: So what do we do with his body? You can't fake a death and see the body running home can you?

ASHER: We can take him to the abandoned well.

GAD: I think merchants still travel that route early in the morning.

RUBEN: Maybe we just leave him there and see what happens.

Joseph enters. The room falls totally silent. He walks in proud, focused, and he pays none of them any mind. He embraces his coat and heads to his sleeping quarters. He bumps into Asher on his way, but doesn't speak.

Judah holds Asher back from getting into a light wrestling match. After the firm correction. He adjusts his plan, once he gets a nod from Judah.

ASHER: Hey brother. I just wanted to be the first to apologize to you for how we've treated you. It must have been hard on you to open up about your dreams in front of us. It is not your fault that you have these silly dreams. What do you say we take a trip tomorrow?

JOSEPH: Really? No games?

Gad walks over with Dan.

GAD: No games.

DAN: We actually got twice as much work done today. So we can all play a little hooky from work for an hour. I mean, don't you agree?

JOSEPH: An hour never hurts. But then we have to get back to work. We need to show Dad we're responsible and can be trusted. Today was hard on him, but he is coming around. I am sure he will be glad to hear that we are going to hangout tomorrow.

GAD: Yeah, but don't mention it to him.

DAN: Yeah, we wouldn't want him to think you are turning into a bad seed.

ASHER: Good point.

RUBEN: We all know how father can get. We all better get some sleep, if we expect to be any good in the morning.

Optional: Video Element time lapse video from night to morning.

Scene Seven

The brothers excluding Ruben are walking down the path.

JOSEPH: Why are y'all walking so fast?

ASHER: We don't have all day do we?

JOESPH: We haven't been gone nearly half an hour I think we can slow down. Ruben is a fast worker.

DAN: When you put it that way. We've been waiting sometime to spend quality time with you.

The brothers stop walking and start standing around Joseph.

GAD: I really like your coat. But I always wondered. Where is my coat? On today, I decided, it doesn't have to be something beyond my grasp. I don't have to worry no more, because I could have a piece of it right now and make my scarf, handkerchief, maybe even a pair of socks.

Gad tears a piece of fabric off the coat. Then Asher takes his coat off of him.

ASHER: We all can.

JOSEPH: Guys stop, do you know how much time and money this cost. And y'all just…I'm telling. Give it back!

DAN: Not this time Joseph.

Dan blocks the path of escape for Joseph. Issachar and Zebulun backs him up.

JOSEPH: Judah, tell him to move.

Asher takes a knife to Joseph.

ASHER: We should just kill him now.

JUDAH: We're not killing anyone. Give me this.

Judah takes the knife.

JUDAH: What we said we were going to do was--

Simeon comes up past Judah and pushes Joseph into the well. The lights can go dark, to transition to focus on the monitors.

Optional: Video Element - Joseph is speaking from within the well or the actor is off stage.

JOSEPH: Come on brothers, this isn't funny. Get me up. I may have jammed my ankle or something.

ASHER: You never thought about us, so why should we now think about you now?

JOSEPH: You don't mean that. Hey. Hey, there are scorpions down here. This isn't funny.

GAD: This is what we all meant to do. Save you from yourself, and us from you. Did you really think we all deserved to serve you?

SIMEON: We all did weigh heavy on killing

you, but it seemed far too harsh. So we are going with plan B. You stay in here and rot. You can thank Ruben for that.

JOSEPH: Judah, Simeon, Levi, Naphtali, Zebulun, Issachar! You all can't hate me this much. Judah, please, I am begging you. You can easily get me out of here…Simeon and Levi you risked your lives to save our sister. You avenged our family before all of Egypt. And you will leave me here now to die? I am your family, and now you turn your back on me? Your own blood, your brother, your kin?

ASHER: There not coming, there keeping watch. We all planned this. Maybe we should put you out of your misery though. Dying by a scorpion bite could be brutal, don't you think?

JOSEPH: Guys, please come on. It's dark down here.

ASHER: Have a good night Joseph. Don't worry, we will get our daily work done just for you after this break.

GAD: You sure know how to work up an appetite.

Asher and Gad walk over to Judah and where

his other brothers are.

JUDAH: Didn't Ruben say not to kill him? Stupid. You want to answer to him? Now what we need to do, is come up with a way to make some money and get him out of that well. That's smarter than leaving him in a hole to rot or him dying from a scorpion bite. This gives us more time to decide if this is what we really want to do. If he dies, there is no turning back.

Asher, Gad, Dan, Zebulun, Judah, Simeon, Levi, Naphtali, and Issachar come running from behind as the Midianite pulls Joseph from the well.

MIDIANITE: Why have you left this young boy in this hole? Don't you know there are scorpions down there?

SIMEON: We know.

MIDIANITE: Well, where is this young man's father?

ISSACHAR: At Home, we are his brothers.

MIDIANITE: I don't believe you. Step aside and I will take him home.

JUDAH: You take one more step and I will drop you where you stand.

JOSEPH: Please don't listen to him. My father can pay you anything you desire. Just bring me home.

JUDAH: You would have to make it there first.

MIDIANITE Very well. My Son, I apologize and I pray you make it home to your father. Forgive me.

The Midianite takes off in a haste.

Naphtali: Maybe this is a sign we should bring him back?

DAN: How do we explain the condition his in Naphtali? Now Simeon go over there with Naphtali and take Joseph. Tie him up, and stand watch this time.

Dan snatches some material from Gad and gives it to Simeon. Naphtali walks Joseph away from the guys.

GAD: Why don't we sell him to the merchants right there?

JUDAH: The Ishmaelites?

ASHER: That's the smartest thing you've said all day.

The Ishmaelite comes on stage and says.

ISHMAELITE: Is he a slave?

DAN: Yes, he is.

ISHMAELITE: How much you want for him? He's not that big? Doesn't look like he does much field work.

GAD: He's a fast learner and comes cheap.

ISHMAELITE: Alright. I will buy him.

The brothers start to exit.

JOSEPH: Simeon, please don't leave me. You're my last chance at getting home.

SIMEON: If only I cared enough to see you back at home brother. So long... Say hi to our uncle and his people for us.

Simeon leaves and hands the rope ties to the Ishmaelite.

ISHMAELITE: Come on slave.

JOSEPH: Ruben!

Joseph and the Ishmaelite exits stage left. The brothers are to the right.

Enters Ruben, running up to his brothers.

RUBEN: Where's Joseph?

ASHER: We sold him.

RUBEN: You what!

GAD: You said to put him in the well and not to kill him—

RUBEN: And then what? I said leave him there!

DAN: We couldn't. There were scorpions in there. He would have died. Ruben, you weren't here, so we had to decide. I thought this was what we all wanted. What's your problem?

RUBEN: Idiots, everyone may hate their little brothers, but they're not crazy enough to sell them into slavery! What is wrong with you guys? Where is your hearts? Do you know what you have done! This kind of news could kill father. Have you thought about that! You and your stupid scarf. How petty have you all been, and fools? Yeah, Joseph wasn't perfect, but he didn't deserve this and you best sure pray the Lord deals with us softly for this.

ASHER: We all wanted a chance.

RUBEN: A chance to betray our brother?

GAD: You were in on this too!

RUBEN: I told you to put him in the well so that I could come back and rescue him. Yes, a part of me enjoyed the fact of him disappearing, but deep down I knew it was wrong. You are all my younger brothers. I am supposed to protect you all—and to know I've lost one, and by my own brothers. What have we done?

Gad tries to hug his brother, but Ruben snatches away.

RUBEN: Don't touch me!

Asher, not missing a beat knows he has to move fast to restore the confidence of the brothers.

ASHER: Look, Ruben, go over there and get ready for your mental breakdown and close up. Right now, we all have to move fast. Dan, go slaughter a goat. Take the largest piece of his coat we have and dip it in the blood. We'll have dad identify the coat and he would assume Joseph is dead. Like we planned. Forget what Ruben is talking about. Some of us ain't built for this. That's just how it is. Ruben, chill out. It's over.

The brothers exit, Ruben tears his shirt.

RUBEN: Lord forgive me. Lord forgive us.

Curtains draw close.

Dance transition _____

Act Two

Scene Eight

Drawn curtains.

Optional: Video Element. Ishmaelites selling Joseph to the Egyptians.

NARRATOR: The Ishmaelites knew they couldn't take Joseph home. They didn't want the trouble or have to provide an explanation for keeping a Hebrew hostage. On their journey they saw Egyptian merchants and they sold Joseph for the same amount they paid. They know the consequence of dabbling in Yah's affairs. They came to reason to wash their hands of it. Joseph was brought to Egypt and purchased by Potiphar and he watched him for weeks on in. He noticed everything he touched the Lord blessed and he sought to promote him.

Curtains open lights fade up.

POTIPHAR: Joseph, I wanted to tell you I am promoting you. I am very pleased with the work you have been doing around here. You are very wise and the favor of your God is evident in your results. I've never seen a slave so useful in my life. If you don't mind me saying?

JOSEPH: Of course I don't, and thank you.

POTIPHAR: I won't lie, in the beginning, I had some doubts. You were very green. You didn't know how to work outside, couldn't clean floors, you were a mess. But I guess that was because it was beneath you.

JOSEPH: That's very kind of you to say.

POTIPHAR: I have something else to say. After this moment, you are more than a slave to me. I am making you the chief in command over all my business so that I may better serve the Pharaoh.

JOSEPH: Thank you Potiphar. I appreciate your acknowledgment. It means the world.

POTIPHAR: I trust you with my life Joseph. You are the most honorable man I know. Slave or Egyptian, that is hard to come by. Keep up the good work!

Potiphar exits. Potiphar's Wife appears from

within the curtains. She slithers out onto the stage. She advances toward Joseph and takes him by surprise.

POTIPHAR'S WIFE: Well aren't you the lucky slave boy. To be purchased by the general, favored in his eyes—in my eyes. Well aren't you going to say thank you?

JOSEPH: Thank you.

POTIPHAR'S WIFE: What a good slave you are. Oh, excuse me chief in command. Does that mean you are not under my control? Under my authority?

She moves closer to him and he gently moves in a different direction ensuring she cannot reach out to touch him.

JOSEPH: My job is to serve Potiphar, to do him good and no harm. He is your husband. Whom I am sure you love and care for very much; and I would never—

POTIPHAR'S WIFE: You assume a lot, Hebrew boy. You know what they say about that.

She gets within arm reach of him and touches him barely.

JOSEPH: I respect your husband even if you won't.

POTIPHAR'S WIFE: Touchy aren't you? I like your feistiness.

JOSEPH: No, loyalty. You like the God in me, trust me you don't like me. You don't care about me, because if you did, you would not try to compromise me. You are a woman that would be a snare to me. Your beauty is undeniable, but my faithfulness to my Elohim is stronger than any beauty, or lust masquerading as anything special.

POTIPHAR'S WIFE: Hmm, seems like there is still more to learn about the mystery Hebrew. I should be celebrated in your eyes not a target. I can do more for you.

JOSEPH: You aren't neither. Your Potiphar's wife and I am his servant. Nothing more. I don't need anything from you. I have more than enough. Your husband has been tremendously generous to me and I would never compromise his trust in me for anything.

POTIPHAR'S WIFE: Why not service everything that belongs to Potiphar?

JOSEPH: Your husband has given me more than my portion. I will respect the one thing he keeps from me, you. But even if I didn't respect him, truly my Father in Heaven I do. He will surely bless me to the ends of the earth, and give me favor as He has been; but only if I don't give Him a reason to remove my covering. I will not bring trouble on my head listening to you. I have to go, I am all done here.

POTIPHAR'S WIFE: Aren't you forgetting something?

JOSEPH: (Clears his throat) May I be excused?

In walks another servant.

POTIPHAR'S WIFE: Yes, Joseph you may go.

Exits Joseph.

POTIPHAR'S WIFE: He is so amazing. His humility, respect, and loyalty only makes me want him more. How dare he deny me? I would be a great catch for him, to think I would consider someone so common is beneath me. It's cute he attempts to shame me. But I always get what I want and I want Joseph.

Song: _____

POTIPHAR'S WIFE: Slave girl, come here. I need someone to indulge my thoughts. I want you to listen, but don't speak.

She nods her head.

POTIPHAR'S WIFE: You catch on quickly. I like you. Now I have to devise a plan to get this man in my hands. He is not like most men, tempted by my good looks, pretty face, irresistible eyes, gorgeous hair, and my power. He is--stubborn. And a loose end I need to tie up and quickly. Can't you see my beauty is suffering because of my pain?

The girl says nothing but just looks at her. She turns her head slighty sideways as she blinks.

POTIPHAR'S WIFE: You can talk now.

SERVANT GIRL: Thank you. If he is different, you cannot do what you normally do to catch him. Maybe pretend to like something he likes to get him to talk to you?

POTIPHAR'S WIFE: Now, that's a good idea. I need to have you talk a bit more often. So here's my plan since you are so smart. I have to get him alone and get him comfortable. What do you think I can do to get that done?

SERVANT GIRL: Maybe get him to make you tea. He cannot tell you no, technically, for something of service. Then give him the right herb and he will see the beauty you have or that his mind pretends you have.

POTIPHAR'S WIFE: I like how you think. Whatever it takes to get him to see me is what I need. I am not used to hearing no, and my body is suffering.

SERVANT GIRL: I can make you a special tea. It will help with your energy temporarily.

POTIPHAR'S WIFE: Give me what you got.

Scene Nine

Joseph is working and wrapping up for the day. In walks Potiphar's Wife.

JOSEPH: I am almost done here.

POTIPHAR'S WIFE: No need to rush. I don't bite, unless of course you want me to?

She comes in and passes behind him. He shifts to leave and she directs her power to make him stay.

POTIPHAR'S WIFE: Sit down, I have not yet excused you. Carry on with your work.

POTIPHAR'S WIFE: Now listen to the voice of reason. Why should you see Potiphar flourish from all the work you have done? Your hard work, mental power, ideas, is why he looks so good. Yet, you play the background never letting people know it is you that should be him. You are the greater man.

JOSEPH: Potiphar is a great man that entrust me with everything in his hands. I am a slave, and he trusts me. I would say that makes him honorable. As to greater, only the Lord can call any man great. Men are simply just men without His blessing.

POTIPHAR'S WIFE: Everything? Hhmm. Except me?

JOSEPH: Correct.

POTIPHAR'S WIFE: Surely every man has the same needs am I to believe you are any different? Every man needs a strong woman by his side. One who can be a friend, a support, and a bit more.

JOSEPH: There are men that fear the Lord.

Those that respect authority, and those still that don't bite the hand that feeds them.

POTIPHAR'S WIFE: That's what impresses me about you. You always have something thought provoking to say. But do you ever relax? You know put the God or Yah stuff down. I respect the gods but we must see and acknowledge human nature. Don't you understand that?

Dance: _____

POTIPHAR'S WIFE: I bet if you just relaxed, you and I would have a great time and become the best of friends.

JOSEPH: This is spiritual don't you understand that? I cannot and will not sleep/be with you. Nor do I want to be close to you. I am not sure what all you have done in your past, but if this does not cease, I will tell Potiphar. I wouldn't want him getting the wrong idea about me. About you…

POTIPHAR'S WIFE: Maybe I should tell him what you tried to do to me? How you tried to pursue me, and waited until all the servants had left to sneaked in here to take advantage of me? Should I call for the guards? Guards! Guards!

JOSEPH: You're crazy.

Joseph exits quickly.

In walks Egyptian Woman One and Two.

POTIPHAR'S WIFE: Ladies how good of you to come and on such short notice.

EGYPTIAN 1: We were on our way to the festival. We didn't see you in the market earlier today grabbing a few things to prepare, so we figured to come by and check on you. See if you wanted to travel with us there. But, if I am honest, you don't have that glow like normal. Maybe you need some of this and a new dress?

POTIPHAR'S WIFE: You silly, dumb and delusional woman. Can't you both tell what is happening to me?

EGYPTIAN 2: I've noticed how washed out and drained you looked. Do you want to talk about it? Can we help you? Are you alright?

POTIPHAR'S WIFE: Can't you see what is happening to me? I am falling ill and the only thing to cure me, is denying me and killing my soul.

EGYPTIAN 2: You mean that young Hebrew running out of here. It would appear he would bring new life to you not have your beauty fade. He is good looking. He can quicken any soul. What is wrong with you?

EGYPTIAN 1: What is wrong with him? Your gorgeous, in shape, have money, class. Why would he deny you?

EGYPTIAN 2: Perhaps he prefers—

POTIPHAR'S WIFE: No, he's interested in women, just not in me.

EGYPTIAN 1: Well I will give him a whirl if he doesn't like you. I am a few years younger than you and that young man is fine!

EGYPTIAN 2: Please, you both are married. He should choose me, the obvious single and best choice.

POTIPHAR'S WIFE: You have slept with most of the guards for jewelry and the afterlife. I am better than you. Both of you. If either one of you takes a foot near him I will take you out/kill you. And I will chase you down in the afterlife and do it again/kill you again.

EGYPTIAN 1: Death wins. He's not that fine.

EGYPTIAN 2: So what are you going to do? At this rate, you will fall dead before you win that Hebrew over. He has principles, morals, and some kind of super power that has you weak.

POTIPHAR'S WIFE: I have my ways. I will get him to sleep/be with me and restore my youth. I will not be outwitted by a child.

In walks Potiphar.

POTIPHAR: Ladies, you both look great.

EGYPTIAN 1 and 2: Thanks, Blessings Potiphar.

POTIPHAR: You mind if I have a moment with my wife?

EGYPTIAN 1: We were just leaving, perfect timing as usual.

POTIPHAR: Honey, I know things have been moving really fast around here lately. And I apologize that I haven't been giving you the attention you deserve. I know life has been hard on you with this sickness, but you can't go out with that on. Remember, we are supposed to the standard for everyone beneath our class.

POTIPHAR'S WIFE: You know I am not feeling my best, Potiphar. I am not focused on a festival, but feeling better and getting well. Right now, I am not up for a festival and entraining people like a show cat.

POTIPHAR: I know the doctors said it may be due to emotional strain on your heart causing you to fall ill. I apologize for my part in this. I hate to see you so unhappy. How can I, as your husband, sit and watch you fade and not be moved to act? Tell me, what can I do? I feel bad I have waited this long to plan something. But my gorgeous feline I am trying.

POTIPHAR'S WIFE: You know I love you, I just need a little time. I want to rest, and see if rest will help restore my energy. You are the best husband a woman could ask for, I think it is just me. But I don't want to drag down your affairs, you must look and be strong for the people. I will be here when you return.

POTIPHAR: I will have Joseph stand guard over the house in my absence. He was set to attend with me, but with the whole city in attendance, I don't want to leave you alone if you need help.

POTIPHAR'S WIFE: You are so carrying and that is why I love you. Go and enjoy yourself. I will be waiting on you when you return.

POTIPHAR: Promise me that you will try to come. I think we could really use this boost. I am missing my wife, and why should I, when she is right here in front of me. Anything you need, you can have. Just tell me, and I am here for you.

POTIPHAR'S WIFE: Just be here for me when I need you, is more than enough.

He goes to give her a kiss and she turns to give him her cheek.

POTIPHAR'S WIFE: Please darling, I am not well.

Out walks Potiphar.

Scene Ten

Potiphar's Wife is dressing up her face utilizing a handheld mirror close to her. She switches out of her old raggedy robe to something alluring, a beautiful dress underneath. She calls for Joseph.

POTIPHAR'S WIFE: Joseph, oh Hebrew. Do you mind coming to my aid to bring me some tea?

Moments later there is a knock at the door. Joseph does not enter but answers from the door.

JOSEPH: Your tea.

She opens the door.

JOSEPH: I am glad to see you have dressed. Potiphar hoped that you would change your mind and attend the festival. I will go and call for your chariot?

POTIPHAR'S WIFE: Silly Hebrew, you will do no such thing. I am not going.

JOSEPH: So you dressed up to stay at home?

POTIPHAR'S WIFE: You are so naive that you are charming. I dressed up for you--I mean me.

JOSEPH: Here is your tea.

POTIPHAR'S WIFE: I was getting dressed to attend with my husband, but the room started to spin and I needed to call for my tea. Please don't leave. And at least, sit my tea down here inside.

Joseph sets the tea down and turns to walk towards the door.

POTIPHAR'S WIFE: Slow down child, I am not going to hurt you. I just want you to talk to me. Please sit.

Potiphar's Wife opens a vile and pours a mixture into Joseph's tea while his back is turned.

JOSEPH: I prefer to stand here and truly I prefer to leave. It is not right for me to be here with the guards and your husband not present.

POTIPHAR'S WIFE: Joseph, please turn around and sit down. Won't you have some tea with me? A sick lady, hurting, and in terrible pain? Maybe you can talk to me about your God? Please, I am desperate for help Joseph. Is it right that you ignore me in my time of need? I mean what would Jesus do?

Joseph sits in the farthest chair closest to the door or stage exit.

JOSEPH: So what would you like to know about my God? How can I pray for you, and please believe I won't be laying on hands.

POTIPHAR'S WIFE: Give me some credit Joseph. I respect the afterlife. Please, tell me something I should know about your God.

JOSEPH: If you know of our history, you likely heard about my grandfather. Abraham, a special servant called by Yah. This would be the first real encounter with my God and your people. You see my grandfather came here and was in awe of what you all had built. He thought, to say his wife was his sister to protect their lives. But the lie caused real problems.

Optional: Video Flashback Pharaoh, Abraham, and Sarah.

JOSEPH: Yes, I know your people know enough about the Hebrew God to know he takes marriage serious, and now your ancestors do too. Thanks for this chat, but I better be leaving.

She encourages him to take the cup, sip, and stay a bit longer.

POTIPHAR'S WIFE: Relax, I am way over here, what can I do to you? Aren't you going to drink your tea? I am sure it is delicious, perfect like you.

JOSEPH: I am actually fine, but thank you.

POTIPHAR'S WIFE: Very well, Joseph do you see how ill I have grown over the past several weeks, months, feels like years of watching you prance, sweat, and work around here?

JOSEPH: No. I make sure no danger comes to you or a person with ill intent. I keep busy, so I am unaware of your struggles. But look, I gotta go and do my job. Thanks for the chat and tea, really.

POTIPHAR'S WIFE: Okay, but wait, just wait. What I am trying to say is I can't help but notice how great your God is to you to keep you young; it's as if you haven't aged a bit. But I guess you have taken my youth and that is why you are fresh and I look, drained. Tell me you desire to see me get well.

JOSEPH: It is my prayer that Yah heals you. I am not a healer, but the God I serve is.

POTIPHAR'S WIFE: And if I told you that I could be healed. All I need is a little participation from you. Kiss me Joseph, and you will see that my love for you is genuine. It's true to my soul. You are the man for me. You have stricken my body with sickness because of your rejection. Don't reject me anymore.

JOSEPH: Woman, I will do no such thing. I am all done with tea, this conversation, please may I be excused.

POTIPHAR'S WIFE: And If I say no?

JOSEPH: I will leave any way.

He gets up to leave and Potiphar's Wife runs up to him and grabs his clothing, she manages to tear a piece of his clothing as he struggles to get away and out the door.

POTIPHAR'S WIFE: Guards! Guards! Please come and help me. My servant has tried to uncover me! Please go and send for Potiphar. The guard heads out in a haste. She sits on her lounge chair and tears the sheer on her dress ever so slightly, then yanks it free. She waits and drinks her tea until she hears footsteps approaching.

POTIPHAR: I was close, I was returning to check on you and I saw a guard running up to me. Wow, you look great, didn't see this energy earlier when I was here. I was hoping you would change your mind, but you look like something is wrong? What is wrong my love?

POTIPHAR'S WIFE: I was thinking to get dressed for you. So that when you arrived, if I were sleep or awake you could rest your eyes on me. But, instead of you coming into our chamber, it was Joseph with tea and I think…I think he tried to drug me. He then tried to tempt me and overtake me, but I yelled for help, and snatched a piece of his garment to defend myself as he wrestled with me.

POTIPHAR: Do tell me, is this true? I know the man Joseph, and I know of his God. Are you sure you have the right man?

POTIPHAR'S WIFE: He looked me in my eyes Potiphar! Am I to believe you love him more than me? That you would trust a slave over your wife? A Hebrew, over an Egyptian?

POTIPHAR: No, no of course not. I'm just stunned, and enraged. My thoughts were scrambled, but I will be right back. I will get to the bottom of this.

POTIPHAR: Guard, come tell me what do you make of this?

GUARD 2: Sir, we were not there and are unsure of the events. What do you think could have happened. Is not your wife's word sufficient enough to condemn the Hebrew?

POET: Poem on what to do.

What do I do?
Do I believe my wife or the Hebrew?
I regret to ask, because I fear the answer.
Do I allow a slave to humble everything I have built?
Do I allow him to steer my ship, changing my course, or do I desert my people?
Is this a battle between the Egyptians and the Hebrew?
I should have never trusted him, or allowed him to become my friend,
But it is hard to see him as a snake in the grass,
Is it him, or just her past?
She is hard to please, likely was never my main squeeze,
A wife to me, but single, free I hope not,
but yes in deed,
I worked so hard is it really about the truth?
My image, my position, or my wife?
I cannot let it be said, I cannot hear what Joseph would say,
Least I doubt and grow to despise my wife,
Would she lie to me twice?
I must do what I dread to do,
Put away the Hebrew,

NARRATOR: The guard with a better view of Joseph's situation replies to the question knowing that either answer is bad for Potiphar. He knows of her comments because of the servant girl, but he swore to secrecy.

GUARD 1: I have more to say, but neither is good sir. If Joseph's garments were snatched from in front, then it is your wife that is at fault, but if from the back, he is at fault.

POTIPHAR: I will go and investigate, please bring him to prison at once.

NARRATOR: Potiphar has Joseph thrown in jail and then goes to visit him. He sees Joseph in jail, sitting alone, clearly thinking of what he did wrong.

POTIPHAR: Joseph, I trusted you with everything of value to me and spared you nothing. I made you the head of my house and never expected you would betray me. It wasn't enough that I gave you my everything you had to try and steal my wife?

JOSEPH: If I am guilty of what you say than I deserve to die right where I sit, but I assure you this is not true. I have been beaten with many stripes for something I did not do, and would not do!

POTIPHAR: So I'm to believe you over my wife? You were always a sensible man Joseph. It's sad you let your talents go to waste like this. I had high hopes for you, for us! How can I go back to my house when you have uncovered me there? Like a slave you had to steal from the master's table.

JOSEPH: I assure you that none of this is true. Didn't you hear the testimony of your own son about your wife's actions towards me? Are not two voices stronger than one? If only you knew of the many times I wanted to come to you.

POTIPHAR: But you didn't. Was it because it was a lie? Did you like my wife and her throwing herself after you so you said nothing?

JOSEPH: No, I wanted to spare you. To protect you. I am a man of logistic, but a man who fears the Lord. I would never cross you or want you to believe I could ever.

POTIPHAR: I used to believe you were honorable. Now you sit her with tattered clothes with the evidence on you body. My wife is scared in her room. Questioning the man I am for sticking up and asking about you? Whatever game you have been playing to replace me Joseph in my home is over now! Enjoy your jail sentence.

NARRATOR: Potiphar backs up to leave, but before he turns, Joseph stands and he goes to him. He goes to Potiphar and he sees that the tear on his clothes are from the front. In shame, Potiphar leaves the prison likely to weep about how he just committed a innocent man to prison. It was a answer that nothing good could come from. Joseph will no longer talks to Potiphar, but to the only God he has ever trusted.

JOSEPH: So this is my life? My life was almost taken. I get pushed in a well, only to be sold into slavery. I am then purchased and seduce by a half crazy lady, and I am the one punished? This can't be my life. This isn't fair. It's not my dream or any dream you have given me! Were my dreams a lie? Were my brothers and family right to say they will not bow to me? Am I the curse? Is the dream, only a dream, never meant to be mine or my reality?

JOSEPH: Lord why am I hear? Do I need to repent? What have I done for you to turn your face from me? Have I offended you? What do I need to do to get out of this place?

MIME Dance: Tell me what do I do? I can't breathe without you, I can live without you. Tye Tribbett.

As the lights turn down and Joseph goes to his cot. He lies there in silence, then soon, he hears a noise at the gate. There is a voice whispering through the bars.

VOICEOVER or VIDEO Element of Potiphar's Wife speaking to Joseph through the bars.

POTIPHAR'S WIFE: Joseph, the unlucky Hebrew. How are you doing, my love? Have you calmed down yet? I know you are upset with me to have to be here away from our home.

Joseph says nothing.

POTIPHAR'S WIFE: Please, hear me. Reply, won't you? Care for me as I care for you. Don't you know Hebrew, I can save you. All you have to do is agree to love me, to be with me, and all will be forgiving. Potiphar doesn't know about us, about me, he will believe what I tell him to. Let me defend you and set you free.

JOSEPH: Woman I will rot her before I turn my back on Yah to be with you.

POTIPHAR'S WIFE: Your God? The one that allowed you to be sold into slavery? The one that allowed you to be put in jail? Come on Joseph, when are you going to wake up? All gods are the same. They use us like pawns in a grand scheme and don't truly love us. We have to love ourselves, and fight for what we want out of life.

JOSEPH: How is that working out for you?

POTIPHAR'S WIFE: I should have known you would remain this stubborn. You will come around. I will visit you every day until you do. You will see like how I do that this God you serve doesn't care about you. You could rot in there.

JOSEPH: This time the well doesn't have scorpions. I will live. Behold the God of the whole earth is able to deliver me from all of your plans. He opens the eyes of the blind, sets free those who are bound, and preserves all strangers who are unacquainted with the land.

POTIPHAR'S WIFE: You will change your mind Hebrew boy.

Potiphar's Wife leaves the prison that day. She returns daily for a span of three months thinking Joseph would change his mind. She brought him food, clothes, and even devised several plans to get him out. Joseph ignored them all and he saw her face fade in beauty with every visit. Whatever had her under a spell, a curse it seemed, was taken a toll on her. She visited Joseph for several months. Then on one of her visits she said.

POTIPHAR'S WIFE: Hebrew, you have been sitting in jail for a year, surely you see this isn't going to end well for you. You will remain here, unless you come with me. I have come to you daily please say you will turn from this foolishness and love me. Just say "yes" to me and all will be well with and for you. Just say "yes."

JOSEPH: That day, year, or moment will never come. Stop visiting me. You are only killing yourself. I can't see you, but I hear in your voice that you still fade. My strength is fine, and I only know to keep praying that my spirit remains. Go live what's left of your life.

NARRATOR: Silence fills the air as time fills the empty room. Joseph is there, praying each day to live in his dreams if he cannot live the dream. If he could sleep more than he was awake, he would. So he planted a tree to keep him company.

INTERMISSION

Song: _____

Talent: _____

Dance: _____

Talent: _____

Comedian: _____

Mime: _____

Talent: _____

Poem: _____

Talent: _____

Dinner/Food: _____

_____

Caterer: _____

Act Two "Continued"

Joseph sits on his cot.

JOSEPH: Okay, I won't fight anymore. If you want me here, here is where I will be. You have the right to give and to take away whatever and whomever you please. But this I know. A Word you speak will and must come to past. A dream you give, according to your power and strength will come to past. So I will continue to believe even though I don't see when nor how it will happen.

JOSEPH: I am but a simple man trying to understand The Almighty and complex Yah. My Elohim I bless you. I encourage myself. I pray you forgive me and appoint my heart to be lifted up.

SONG: _____

The CUP BEARER and the BAKER enter.

VOICE OVER or Video Element- The prison guard, cup bearer, and baker walk to the prison. The guard throws the two of them inside.

PRISON GUARD: Joseph be sure to keep an eye on these two.

JOSEPH: Hey, how's it going?

BAKER: What are you cheery for? Don't you know you are in a prison?

JOSEPH: Physically yes, but it's not always where you see yourself, but where you can see yourself in the end because of purpose, destiny.

BAKER: I don't understand any of that but I know the Pharaoh threw us down here and he didn't seem too eager to get us out. Prison for me doesn't seem like part of my destiny as much as it is part of my reality.

JOSEPH: I see.

CUP BEARER: I am not sure why I am here. I was doing my job servicing the Pharaoh and ended up here. Not too sure if I should get worried yet. I know I didn't do anything wrong.

BAKER: Dummy don't you get it. They think you tried to kill the Pharaoh. Haven't you been paying attention to the previous cup bearers who came here to die. We're going to die in here!

CUP BEARER: You may die in here, but I'm not dying in here. I didn't do anything wrong.

BAKER: You don't have to, to die. It's all about what they believe. Don't you get it? If they think you are guilty, you are as good as dead.

JOSEPH: Okay stop, you're scaring him. I am sure if you are innocent you will be re-appointed. Try and relax. How long are you here for?

CUP BEARER: Only three days. We await the feast when we will be judged.

JOSEPH: Then pray to your god and I will pray to mine concerning you both.

BAKER: The gods care for no one. They don't care if we live or die.

JOSEPH: True. But my God is not yours. He is not of the sun, trees, moon, this or anything you have ever seen—that's what makes Him different.

CUP BEARER: You can pray for me. I need all the help I can get. I don't want to die. Hey, but what's your name anyway?

JOSEPH: Yeah, okay bet. My name's Joseph. Why don't you both lay down and rest and I will pray.

The men sit down to rest.

JOSEPH: Father, these men are troubled. Ease their spirits. Reveal to them their future and bring peace to their mind, body, and spirit. Elohim You are all knowing and nothing escapes your eyes, memory, or reach.

The baker wakes up screaming.

BAKER: Ahhh.

JOSEPH: Calm down you're here. Wake up.

Joseph shakes the baker awake. The Cup Bearer is still sound asleep with a smile on his face. The baker looks over and asks Joseph.

BAKER: What is he smiling for?

The baker goes over to the Cup Bearer and shakes him awake aggressively.

BAKER: Wake up, why are you smiling?

CUP BEARER: Because I had a dream. Why

are you frantic?

BAKER: Because I too had a dream (Martin Luther King Voice)?

JOSEPH: You guys want to share your dreams?

BAKER: Who are you that we should share our dreams? You Houdini, a magician or something? I knew you had a edge to you like you deal with mystic beings or something.

JOSEPH: Interpretations of dreams belongs to The One and TRUE God, Yahweh. I am no psychic, magician, or a person dealing with mystic beings. Yah tells me what your dreams mean and I simply tell you what He says.

CUP BEARER: Alright dream reader, I want to know what my dream meant. In my dream, I saw a vine in front of me, and on the vine were three branches. As soon as it budded, it blossomed, and its clusters ripened into grapes. Pharaoh's cup was in my hand, and I took the grapes, squeezed them into Pharaoh's cup and put the cup in his hand.

Joseph takes a moment to reflect on the dream and does a quick internal prayer. After another moment of pause, he begins to speak.

JOSEPH: Your dream is simple. This is what it means. The three branches are three days. Within three days Pharaoh will lift up your head and restore you to your position, and you will put Pharaoh's cup in his hand, just as you used to do when you were his Cup Bearer.

JOSEPH: Can I ask of you this one favor?

CUP BEARER: Sure anything!

JOSEPH: When all goes well with you, remember me and show me kindness; mention me to Pharaoh and get me out of this prison. I was forcibly carried off from the land of the Hebrews, and even here, I have done nothing to deserve being put in a dungeon.

But before the cup bearer could speak, the Baker interrupts him.

BAKER: Alright. Alright, I will surely remember you, too. I too had a dream: On my head were three baskets of bread. In the top basket were all kinds of baked goods for Pharaoh, but the birds were eating them out of the basket on my head. What do you make of that?

Joseph takes another pause. Internally prays and then is slow to speak.

JOSEPH: Well, this is what it means. The three baskets are three days. Within three days Pharaoh will lift off your head and impale your body on a pole. And the birds will eat away at your flesh.

BAKER: Are you sure man? Rub your eyes, take two deep breaths, and wake up again. I think you maybe a little woozy or something. Or maybe you can call out to your God and ask Him to give me favor, change my fate?

JOSEPH: I can't change His mind only tell you what He said. My Elohim is the same God and He changes not. I am sorry man, but you better settle your issues and get right with whatever god or afterlife is next in line for you.

BAKER: This is crazy. You don't know anything. Pretty desperate of us to ask you to interpret our dreams. If you were so in tune with God, why are you here?

CUP BEARER: Just because you don't like your dream's meaning, doesn't mean you beat this man up.

BAKER: You're only saying that because you don't die in yours!

CUP BEARER: Like you said, pretty desperate for us to ask him to reveal the future. Relax, maybe you will live?

BAKER: Yeah, and maybe not. I never got a chance to talk to my wife, my kids…

JOSEPH: Pray while there is still time. For tomorrow isn't promised.

BAKER: Where did they find you?

JOSEPH: I am not of this land. I come from the land of the Hebrews.

BAKER: Figures. Man, I'm hungry. When do we got something to eat?

JOSEPH: Food here comes every few days. Your next meal maybe at the Pharaoh's feast. Rest up and preserve your strength.

BAKER: Great. I don't get a last meal. Last words to my family. I'm just going to die? Right?

Joseph looks down at the ground and says nothing. The Cup Bearer looks in the other direction. The baker hangs his head low.

BAKER: I am not guilty of doing anything wrong. I did what I needed to do to support my family. I am sure your God doesn't allow good men to die? If He does, HE is no better then the gods. I refuse to bow down and worship any god that doesn't care about me. About my family, heck about my food! So if hell is my home I guess I am ready! But I am going to dream good thoughts tonight, and right now.

The baker positions himself to rest. But he is tossing and turning in his sleep.

FADE OUT

The lights dim.

Scene Eleven

The stage is adorn to resemble a chief's table. The table is arrayed with things. And the Pharaoh's chair is positioned on the stage. He has two children fanning him on his left and his right. Guards stand guard at the doors, or corners of the room/stage.

The Pharaoh gets up from his seat to address the AUDIENCE.

PHARAOH: Today is the great feast and I welcome you all into my gates and my presence. As you know we have business to attend during this feast. I see that you all are some very fine, wise, knowledgeable people with rapport throughout the lands. Allow me to explain how I shall request your help. For many of you that are unaware, I imprisoned two men for suspicious behavior three days passed. On today, before you, they will be judged.

PHARAOH: Do you mind helping me?

Audience: Response if not, the Narrator: "Of course they're ready. They just need one more chance, Pharaoh. Audience, are you all ready to do a judging?" Response: "Yes"

PHARAOH: Let's do it. But first it is customary that I be entertained to be made merry before such judgments can or should take place. You don't ever want to judge when I'm in ill spirits. I may be as ruthless as I feel. So I ask, who out there can entertain me and keep me in good spirits?

If no response, "Don't all speak at once, surly someone out there is able, confident—"

SINGER: I can.

PHARAOH: Very well. Take the mic and don't disappoint! I don't take too well to disappointment. Your life and theirs rest in your hands, no pressure I am sure.

SINGER: Yes, no pressure at all almighty Pharaoh. SONG. (Selected singer to be included in the show.)

SONG: _____

PHARAOH: I am very well pleased. You shall receive a reward from Pharaoh. I am now ready to judge. Bring them out.

The Baker and Cup Bearer are brought before Pharaoh.

PHARAOH: Now Cup Bearer plead your case.

CUP BEARER: Mighty Pharaoh, I know you know how much I do enjoy serving and bearing your cup. I have proved most trusted, most faithful, to you and to your wellbeing. I have drank from your cup knowing death may be imminent, but I serve you with great honor. And it is very much my desire to return to continue to serve you and whatever may have been discovered about my actions, will prove my innocents from any wrong doing against you and to the throne.

PHARAOH: Audience, what do you say about this plea? Sincere or insincere? Say "Yes," if you believe the Cup Bearer is sincere, and if insincere, say "no." On the count of three, I want to hear how you judge. One, two, three, let's hear your answer?

Audience: Response, if no response, repeat. If the wrong answer, say "Come one. You have read the Bible. Is he sincere or insincere?" If they answer but are too low, say, "Great you have read the Bible, now speak louder and with confidence."

PHARAOH: Very well, I have weighed your responses, and because of proof submitted I take him to be sincere. Cup Bearer you have been vindicated of any accused transgressions and I would like to re-appoint you back to my side.

CUP BEARER: Oh, thank you mighty Pharaoh!

PHARAOH: Baker it is now your turn to come before me and plead your case.

BAKER: Mighty Pharaoh bless you greatly. I have been baking for you for a few years and

I very much enjoy my job. I am faithful, kind, love good food, and would like very much to keep cooking tasty bites for you and your house.

PHARAOH: This is not what I have heard.

BAKER: The other cooks in the kitchen don't know fine dining. I know great cooking. I have trained with the best, (list four prominently known chiefs). So, yes, I may throw away food with blemishes and be extremely choosy with ingredients. I only serve the finest foods to you mighty Pharaoh.

PHARAOH: And about the bribes you take.

BAKER: (Clears his throat and his voice goes to a higher pitch.) Excuse me bribes? I don't know anything about that. I mean like I said, I only serve you the best. I don't take strange ingredients. I am—

PHARAOH: Again, not what I have heard, but I am going to ask my guest how should I judge. They know the Bible, and the truth of the matter. Do you all believe he is sincere in his desire to serve me? "Yes" for sincere or "no" for insincere. Shout it out!

Audience Response: If no response encourage response.

PHARAOH: I believe most of you perhaps know what I now believe. You are the guilty party responsible for the attempt to take my life by poisoning, and you will not return to bake or cook for me or anyone beyond this date. Today, you will die, and because I am in good spirits, I will sentence you to a quick death. Guards take him away.

The guards take him into their arms and begin to drag him off stage.

BAKER: No, no, please. I didn't mean it. I can do better. It wasn't my fault. That dang Joseph set me up!

PHARAOH: Now, let's party and enjoy this festival.

Dance performance _____

Mime Performance _____

Poem _____

Fade to BLACK.

Scene Twelve

NARRATOR: Time has passed, years had passed. The kingdom is currently having a problem with the Pharaoh sleeping. His dreams are troubling him and he is looking for someone to help him ease his worrying; but to date he has found no one.

The Pharaoh is sitting in his royal chair and he is talking to Potiphar.

PHARAOH: I am sorry Potiphar. I am struggling to focus. I haven't been sleeping.

POTIPHAR: Tell me my Pharaoh, what troubles you?

PHARAOH: I am having a dream that I don't want to repeat, for fear it will come to past.

POTIPHAR: This must be a pretty serious dream?

PHARAOH: I am afraid it is. I gave it to the hands of the magicians, and none of them could make sense of it. Everything they said just made me angry and I ordered them to be feed to the lions for failing me. I was not in good spirits.

POTIPHAR: Let me see what I can do to help, if anything. You can trust me to help you, mighty Pharaoh.

FADE UP.

Potiphar is sitting on his chair and he looks deep in thought. He is not speaking just staring with intense emotion. His wife comes up around him and tries to usher him out of his mood.

POTIPHAR WIFE'S: Potiphar, what troubles you?

POTIPHAR: I hear the Pharaoh's need and I know the man that can help. But how can I trust a man that betrayed me? After all I did, we did for him? He tried to touch the only thing I withheld from him. How can I bring a man like that anywhere near the Pharaoh? He was a powerful man of God in his season, but he became corrupt. Jealous of me. How can I trust him to be this close to Pharaoh and not double cross me?

POTIPHAR WIFE'S: What man are you talking about?

POTIPHAR: Joseph, has it really been that

long that you have forgotten him?

POTIPHAR WIFE'S: Yes, I remember him, but Potiphar that happened 12 years ago. I've grown to forgive him and I am able to put aside the past if that will help Mighty Pharaoh. I believe we are strong enough to do this together.

POTIPHAR: How can I put this behind me, and forgive him? I had him in my house. He was faithful to me and I thought he was a righteous man. But when he grew comfortable, he turned and bit the hand that fed him, honored him, and clothed him as one of their own. He had everything; but that wasn't enough and he wanted more—He wanted you. I have been living 12 years and 3 months, 27 days, and 6 hours with this shame and guilt of putting you endanger. I cannot risk my life, on this Hebrew to cost me anymore than he has—

POTIPHAR WIFE'S: Joseph was a good man to this family and perhaps he just made a mistake. He was young. Aren't we raised to forgive to improve our state of being in the afterlife?

POTIPHAR: Doesn't he know stealing a man's wife no matter your god is punishable by death? He should be glad we didn't order him to be put to death. I showed him mercy, but perhaps I shouldn't have? I pushed for it, but with the circumstances, I couldn't enforce it.

POTIPHAR WIFE'S: You don't mean that.

POTIPHAR: Of course I do. That Joseph is a fraud. You, you were so angry with me. What man--husband would I be if I couldn't defend my wife? If you ask me, he needs 12 more years for what he has done. I tell you, I should--

POTIPHAR WIFE'S: Look Potiphar. I think I need to tell you this and honestly I should have a long time ago. I felt that you always knew and you came to forgive me. Joseph is not the man I made him out to be. He is faithful to you and to this house, even long after he left this place. He followed you without question. It was I that tempted Joseph.

A moment goes by and Potiphar doesn't make a sound, make a move, he just sits there with a blank stare on his face. Potiphar's wife moves closer to ensure he hears her and he responds to her closeness by recoiling his arm.

POTIPHAR WIFE'S: Did you hear what I said Potiphar?

POTIPHAR: Is it true that the guards saw you at the prison?

POTIPHAR WIFE'S: That is also true.

POTIPHAR: Woman, you allowed me to put a man in jail and have him sit there for all this time because you wanted to protect your nasty self? So this is what has been eating you alive? This is why your health is fading and you are a shadow of yourself? The gods have judged you and I stayed with you. I wanted to believe you so badly, but I knew you were trash and what I didn't have the heart to do, it looks like the Hebrew God permitted it for me. You look like hell/crap.

POTIPHAR WIFE'S: Why do you say it like that? Why are you being so vile to me?

POTIPHAR: To think the miracle of our two year old speaking to me about you and Joseph was a lie, you made me doubt him. I thought our son was bewitched, but it was the Hebrew God using my own son to tell me about the treacherous wife I have had for all of these years. You lucky I am still calm, but I'm going to deal with this later. This isn't over for you. I had the feeling, and I think I knew, but you didn't say it, so I could deny it. Now I have to face my choice and mistakes.

Potiphar rushes out of the house.

Scene Thirteen

Potiphar arrives at the jail and request the Guard to let him in.

Enters Potiphar to Joseph cell.

POTIPHAR: Joseph?

JOSEPH: I am here, Potiphar.

POTIPHAR: I need to ask you a favor.

JOSEPH: Anything.

POTIPHAR: I would like to ask you to meet with the Pharaoh to interpret his dream. Do you think you can do it?

JOSEPH: I know my Elohim is faithful to explain any dream. Dream interpretations belong to Him alone. Should we go at once?

POTIPHAR: Yes. But wait. I need to tell you something.

JOSEPH: Sure.

POTIPHAR: I need to tell you I am sorry for sending you in here. She told me what happened and I am embarrassed, hurt.

JOSEPH: Don't be.

POTIPHAR: I am because a part of me thought it was her, but I couldn't bring myself to believe that. What I want to say is she clearly isn't the woman for me because when she had me, she chose to chase you. You're a great man and I trust and hope someday I can call you friend.

JOSEPH: I would have done the same. Thanks for coming here. Over the years, I thought of what I would say, or do, if I ever saw you again. The only thing in my heart to say is, "Friend, I forgive you."

The two shake and head out the door together.

Scene Fourteen

The Pharaoh is sitting on his throne and the Cup Bearer is close by his side. The children are fanning them with leaves and the guards are present.

PHARAOH: It is great I spared your life some years ago. You have been so helpful to me as of late.

CUP BEARER: It was a great day when I was able to serve by your side again. It is my pleasure to remain. But Pharaoh, if I can ask, you don't look well. Should I fetch medicine for you?

PHARAOH: No. I am not sick.

CUP BEARER: May I ask, what's up? You don't seem like yourself.

PHARAOH: Yes, I am not myself lately. I am disturbed because of a dream I had just last night. I've asked around so that I may understand it, but I haven't been able to find a soul to interpret it. Now, I refuse to share it, but want the right dreamer to prove he can help me. Too many have failed.

CUP BEARER: Surely there is someone that can shed light. Have you tried all the magicians?

PHARAOH: Every last one in the Kingdom. Still no luck.

CUP BEARER: I know a man. I had a dream while in the dungeon and he gave me the meaning of my dream. I am ashamed to have forgotten about him, and not have spoken about him sooner. He gave me confidence and told me the entire truth before the feast; that I would be back bearing your cup, and here I am.

PHARAOH: Send for this man.

Enters Potiphar and Joseph.

POTIPHAR: Mighty Pharaoh, should I return later?

PHARAOH: No, it's fine. I was just speaking about this dream I had. I've been looking for someone to explain it to me, but I have found a man and would like to send for him. Can you help me with this?

POTIPHAR: The man you are looking for is Joseph. I brought him with me.

PHARAOH: So, you are the man I hear who can interpret my dream?

JOSEPH: My Elohim knows all dreams, and He will give you peace great Pharaoh.

PHARAOH: Very well. What do you seek for your help? Compensation, freedom?

JOSEPH: My life is in the hands of Yahweh. I go where he sends me and serve how He permits. I am only here to help you mighty Pharaoh.

The Pharaoh studies his face and believes him to be sincere.

PHARAOH: Alright. I had two dreams. The first, seven cows were feeding near the river. They were healthy, full, fat; and shortly after 7 more cows emerged and they were thin, gauntly, and unhealthy. The seven unhealthy cows consumed the fat healthy cows.

PHARAOH: The second dream was about corn. I had seven ears of corn that sprung up, healthy, the stalk was full and then there were seven ears of corn that sprung that were not. The seven unhealthy stalks that withered consumed the healthy stalks. And after this I woke up.

Joseph takes a pause and does an internal prayer. He then hears a response as the Pharaoh looks on with expectancy.

JOSEPH: Your two dreams have the same message. Yahweh is showing you what is to come as a warning. The seven healthy cows, stalks, represent seven years of plenty. The seven unhealthy cows, withered stalks, represent seven years of famine. You dreamed this twice because it will surely come to past.

PHARAOH: I see. Did your God tell you what we should do about this?

JOSEPH: No, at least not exactly. But if you will permit me, I have a suggestion. The famine will be great and the years of plenty will be forgotten because it will be so great. You must set a trustworthy man who is wise and knowledgeable to help store food during the years of plenty to be able to sustain the kingdom during the years of famine.

PHARAOH: I don't know any man that has the God that you have. No one I know, can do what you just did. You are the only that I know with the Spirit. So, I must say that you are the best for the job. You will be first in command, ruling my kingdom, and you will only come second to me.

JOSEPH: Gracious king, may you live forever.

PHARAOH: I am not done. You will have a bride worthy of your royal office. I will give you the beautiful daughter of On, and I will give you your own living quarters and wealth. Whatever you need for your job, just name it, and you shall surely have it.

JOSEPH: As you have said, that it will be. Thank you, Pharaoh.

PHARAOH: It is I who should be thanking you and the God that you serve. I presume I will have great sleep this night. Thanks for making my spirit merry.

NARRATOR: What's for you is for you. Time might have you think it is canceled, but trust, that it will only delay but never cancel out. The enemy hopes you will stop believing and hoping for it--don't lose faith or courage. Don't give up on God because He will not give up on you. He is always able!

Fade to Black

NARRATOR: Later that day, Joseph could not contain his joy. He was pulled from the prison and put in the best housing, given the best food, and had a beautiful wife. What he thought he had missed or was robbed of having, was repaid to him with interest. The Father recovered it all--including his time.

JOSEPH: (Aside) Oh great redeemer. My Elohim, my soul rejoices. You have been faithful to me in the midst of my pain, and Lord I thank you. I bless your Holy and mighty name. You are alpha, omega, above, and not beneath. I thank you for your faithfulness and love for a man like me. Continue to be with me and keep my ear to hear You, and keep my heart willing to serve You. May my family know that all is wealth with my soul. Keep them during the years of plenty and famine.

FADE to BLACK.

POET:
Times were changing for sure,
Joseph went from being poor to having things galore,
He thought he was forgotten but realized, he was in the best hands, and part of the Master's plan,
When the Cup Bearer came, he forgot the one he swore to remember,
At first it made him bitter until he remembered,
It is not people who saved or redeemed him,
It has always been the Good Lord, God, Almighty.
The one who raised him, calling him forth

from his mother's belly,
Was there with him in Potiphar's house, the prison, to the palace.
When you are heartbroken and searching for the residue of Yah in your world,
Learn like Joseph, He will never leave nor forsake you.
He will be there, making a way, holding and protecting you,
Keeping you for the season and time such as this, where your gift cannot be missed.

Act Three

Scene Fifteen

Video Element: Time lapse of 14 years. The Egyptians were planting, seeding, harvesting, and gathering during the years of plenty.

NARRATOR: Fourteen years has passed. Under the wise guidance of Joseph, the people worked smart, and the Pharaoh gathered much into his barns. The seven years of plenty were bountiful and the wise, stored up grain and food for the seven years of drought. Not everyone got the message, but those who had a ear to hear, heard the warning.

NARRATOR: But even those who did, they were not all able to make it out of the seven years of brutal famine. Many of the Egyptians had to sell their land and things to the Pharaoh to survive. But they weren't the only ones suffering. The neighboring countries and people were suffering even as far out as the land of the Hebrews. The world was coming to trade with Egypt, and all had to meet and negotiate with

Joseph.

NARRATOR: Back in the land of the Hebrews, Joseph's brothers tell their father of their daily struggles. The father and the men are gathered at the table to give reports to Israel about the land.

RUBEN: I've searched all along the bank and I found nothing.

GAD: I've also searched and came up empty.

ASHER: I think you know what I am going to say. Nada.

ISRAEL: Are you sure we are looking in the right places?

RUBEN: The land has been barren for awhile dad. I have been warning you that this day might come sooner than later.

ASHER: I can tell you Dad, there is nothing out there but some thistles and briers, or empty branches.

GAD: The dirt is even as dry as a bone. Nothing can grow in this. It is not just that there has been no rain, or the harvest has been few, the earth seems to have shut off. Nothing can grow like this and I don't know for how long we can go on like this, Dad.

ISRAEL: So you are telling me, we are out of options?

ASHER, GAD, RUBEN: Yes.

ISRAEL: I have been hearing that grain and food is in Egypt. If that is true, we're looking in the wrong places. If we want to feed our family we must go to Egypt. They may be the only one who has food.

RUBEN: Dad, I can go.

DAN: I will go to.

ISRAEL: Good, I will need you all to go to ensure we get as much grain as possible to feed everyone for as long as possible. If this famine is as bad as you say it is Gad, we can't take any chances.

BENJAMIN: We all get to go father?

ISRAEL: Not you, your brothers can handle it. I need you here to help.

BENJAMIN: But Dad, I need to do something. I have a wife and family also to protect like my brothers. Trust me to go and help.

ASHER: No, Dad is right. You are needed here.

GAD: We need someone here to keep things going while we are out. We all trust you Benjamin.

ISRAEL: You are needed here. I need you here. If anything were to happen to you, I couldn't bare it. Please, stay with me.

BENJAMIN: Of course.

DAN: We'll leave at once and be back soon.

ISRAEL: Take sacks of money and make sure you bring extra. I know things can get crazy when the world doesn't have food. Try and negotiate for as much as you can get and spare no expense.

RUBEN: We understand Dad.

ISRAEL: Please Asher, Ruben, keep an eye out for everyone. Especially Judah, Simeon, and Levi. You know how they can be and we can't have their hot heads costing us.

ASHER: Of course, Dad. We won't let you down.

RUBEN: I will make sure of it and protect them all with my life.

They exit.

BENJAMIN: Dad, I love you, and my brothers do too. We want what's best for you, and at some point, I will have to become a man who contributes to this family.

ISRAEL: Benjamin, you are a wonderful man. You give to this family as a father, husband, and uncle. You are a great son to me. I couldn't ask for more.

BENJAMIN: But I can do more. Dad, I am okay. I am not as strong as Judah, but I am not weak. I might be the youngest, but I pray that you won't always have an excuse to keep me so close.

ISRAEL: Benjamin, you are all I have left--look I know you don't understand my hurt, or my pain. Your brothers don't either, but they try and that's all I can ask. I have lost a wife and a son, I will not lose you too.

BENJAMIN: But Dad, I am not a child you have to worry about. I know Yah, I have my brothers, and I have your wisdom. Don't you think that is enough?

ISRAEL: It will be when the time comes. Right now, you stay put.

BENJAMIN: Fine, Dad. But know that things will not always be like this. You will have to let me grow up and step up for this family. I love who I am, and I want to do my part. You got to trust that I can do that when the time comes.

The room is filled with silence. Benjamin exits.

ISRAEL: Father, there are no secrets I keep from you. You are the only who knows my heart and can see what I cannot. May you keep charge over my sons as they travel. May you keep them safe, and give them favor with the Egyptians to acquire enough food to feed our families. Thank you, Father, for helping us during this famine. Please keep providing a way of escape for my family. Please heal my heart for those departed, Rachel and Joseph.

ISRAEL: I know I cannot hold on to Benjamin forever, but allow me to hold him close. Allow me to keep him safe from the dangers that lurk outside. May his brothers keep him safe and be honorable to one another. My Heavenly Father, I trust you have heard my prayer and have sealed it. In the name of the Father, Yahweh, I trust.

Scene Sixteen

The brothers are packing and Benjamin comes into the room.

BENJAMIN: Brothers, I am sadden I cannot go with you. I know how important this mission is for all of us.

JUDAH: Do you know how important you are here?

BENJAMIN: So important that dad wants to keep me tucked in the house. I am not a child.

LEVI: Go easy on Dad. He is trying, and I for one can see how Yah will change his heart. Give him time.

BENJAMIN: How much time? I will be a old man before he will let me leave home. I want to explore the world and really contribute to this family.

SIMEON: How much do you think this family could do without Israel, our father to nations?

LEVI: Our family is large, and our purpose is great. We could not do this without you here. You might feel like a small part, but you are a bigger part to the puzzle than you think. What's for You is For You. You can't miss it, and it can't be taken from you.

JUDAH: If your older brother was here, Joseph, he would say something like that, wouldn't he?

SIMEON: He was always ahead of his time. He was a real old soul like you.

LEVI: Don't reject humble beginnings or doubt your timing or purpose. No matter how small a toe is, you need all ten to balance the whole body. You might be small, but you are so necessary. You are needed here for more reasons than one.

BENJAMIN: Really? You guys are not just saying that to make me feel better?

SIMEON: We nearly lost dad after Joseph, we cannot have him risk going through another loss in his mind like that. He is a power source for our family,

and we need him going. Do you understand what that means?

JUDAH: It means, that with you in place, you are able to uphold our family to keep us going forward. We are all part of the same vine.

LEVI: Part of the same vine. Plus, we can't leave our women uncovered for some thugs to come and swoop in, in our absents. Dad will give them a run for their money, but you, you will defend us like a king.

BENJAMIN: I understand. Sorry about being in my own head.

SIMEON: Don't apologize, that's what brothers are here for.

Optional: Video Element: Issachar and Zebulun are packing up the bags on the camels and wagons. The ten brothers are traveling to Egypt.

NARRATOR: The sons arrive into the presence of Joseph unaware that he is who they must meet to buy and negotiate grain and food for their families.

NARRATOR: Joseph sat on his throne and his eyes spotted his 10 brothers. They were moving as a group, staying close together and being mindful of those around them. It blessed Joseph's heart to see them as they paid their respects to the guards, and approach him.

JOSEPH: Where do you come from and what do you want?

They bowed down before him

ASHER: I am Asher, we come from the Land of Canaan and we've come to buy food.

JOSEPH: I don't believe you. You are spies are you not?

GAD: Mighty Pharaoh I am Gad, I assure you we are not spies, but are 12 brothers from the land of Canaan here to buy food.

JOSEPH: Surely you are spies sent here to scope out the land. I don't see 12 brothers, I see ten spies here to scope out the land.

RUBEN: No Pharoah, I am Ruben, and also here with us is Dan, Judah, Naphtali, Levi, Simeon, Zebulon, Issachar, Benjamin is our youngest brother and he is with our father.

DAN: There is one that is no longer with us, but we are all born of one father Israel and we are from the land of Canaan.

JOSEPH: And what of your fathers? Who are they?

LEVI: We are descendants of Abraham, Issac, and Jacob, who is known as Israel.

JOSEPH: Why does the name Abraham sound familiar?

NAPHTALI: Our grandfather was here before with his wife Sarah. He lied and said she was his sister and caused trouble for the Egyptians.

JOSEPH: Didn't he do that twice?

SIMEON: I know how this might look, but we are not here for war or trouble. Only to buy food.

JOSEPH: Are you not the brothers who pursued 5 kings in a single battle for your sister's virtue?

JUDAH: Yes we are. But like we said, we are not here as spies. We just want to buy food for a fair price and return home to our father and families.

RUBEN: What my brother is trying to say, we have brought money as requested by our father to pay the right price for food. We understand you might be the only outlet in our region. Our family would be grateful to you, if you would sell us grain.

JOSEPH: I've heard enough. By the Pharaoh you are all liars unless you can show me your youngest brother. You can leave a brother here with me to then go fetch your youngest brother. And then will I believe you are not spies.

JOSEPH: But, because I am still not certain if I should trust you all, I will put you all in jail for three days to investigate your coming here. If I find no fault, I will send you home to retrieve your youngest brother. Then I might be more open to believe you are all not spies, then. Guards!

The royal guards come and stand near the brothers.

JUDAH: You really think we cannot take them all, Ruben?

RUBEN: Dad told me to keep you calm.

LEVI: I will be calm for now, but if this goes side ways, you already know what's going to happen.

SIMEON: I am with you.

ASHER: Brothers, fall back. We good. We sit and wait three days, then we do what we have to do to save our families.

The brothers walk with the guards and they don't resist.

Fade to black

NARRATOR: Three days later. The brothers are back in front of Joseph.

JOSEPH: I almost believe you may not be spies, for now. But to prove I am correct, one of you must remain in your prison until all of your brothers come to let you out. You must all return home and bring back your youngest brother, and I will release the one that stays behind trusting you are not spies.

JOSEPH: Take a moment to speak among yourselves for who will remain.

RUBEN: I knew we should have never brought

innocent blood on our heads. Asher, Gad, Dan didn't I warn you? Now if Benjamin's blood is required--truly this is punishment for what we did to Joseph.

ASHER: I will stay. This is mostly on me.

DAN: No, I should stay. I was just as guilty.

GAD: I will stay, that dang coat just kept ringing in my head. I knew I was meant to be fly, but my own desires blinded me.

NARRATOR: Watching the brothers argue over who wanted to stay started to pull on Joseph's heart strings. He couldn't watch them any more and wanted the evidence of how they truly felt about each other, and the brother, him, that was no more.

JOSEPH: I will take Simeon. The rest of you can leave and bring back your youngest brother. When you return, I will release Simeon, believe you are not spies, and be open to trade with you. You may all leave now.

The guards move in to take away Simeon who goes with them without a cry for help.

SIMEON: Brothers. I will see you soon. Tell my

wives and family I will see them soon. And to dad, tell him not to worry. I will be fine. Simeon is marched out. The brothers exit and Joseph sends everyone out.

JOSEPH: Oh Father. My father lives and is well. How I long to see him and my family again. To hold them, and tell them I love them. But have they really changed? Are they kinder to my baby brother than to me?

The lights deem.

JOSEPH: (weeping) Lord how long will I bear this secret? How long before I see my father? How much have they missed me or do they celebrate my untimely exit? Why do I feel like I do? I should be past all of this, but here I am a grown and powerful man, crying about the past.

Fade to black.

SONG or Dance transition _____

Scene Seventeen

In the room of Israel. The sons arrive home to their father. The sons enter to give him their report and answer about the matter ahead.

ISRAEL: It took some time for you all to go and return. Was there a issue?

JUDAH: We found our way there fine. We did meet with their second in charge to negotiate food, but there was a problem.

ISRAEL: What kind of problem?

ASHER: We got asked a lot of questions about our travels and why we were truly there.

GAD: They took us as spies.

ISRAEL: Spies?

DAN: Yeah, Dad. Their Second in command was so convinced that he had us jailed for three days to prove our innocence.

ISRAEL: And what now?

LEVI: He was not fully convinced. We had to prove our family history and the sincerity of our story by fulfilling a request.

ISRAEL: What kind of request?

ISSACHAR: He wants us to prove that there is in fact 11 brothers and not ten. He counted and asked about Joseph.

ISRAEL: What does this mean?

ZEBULUN: It means we have to go back and prove we are not spies.

ISRAEL: So did we buy any food or do we have to wait?

RUBEN: We got food but father when we checked our sacks we found our money replaced.

ASHER: I had nothing to do with it.

ISRAEL: Of course not. When you go back you need to bring double the portion.

RUBEN: Father, there is one more thing I must tell you.

ISRAEL: Yeah, one minute. Where is Simeon?

RUBEN: That's part of what I wanted to tell you.

DAN: We had to leave him behind.

ISRAEL: WHAT?

GAD: The Pharaoh took us to be spies and said we had to leave Simeon behind in prison and return with Benjamin to free him. He won't stop believing we are spies without him.

ISRAEL: Wait what? Are you trying to put me in an early grave? Benjamin is not leaving this house.

RUBEN: I promise there will come no harm to Benjamin.

ISRAEL: And what can be said of Simeon?

ASHER: Father we had no choice but to leave him. I volunteered but the Pharaoh didn't take me, or Gad, Dan and the others.

ISRAEL: So, I send you to get food and I am left with one less son and now you want a third? I assure you Benjamin will not leave my side.

RUBEN: Father we cannot return without him. We cannot buy food without Benjamin coming with us. I promise you father, on the life of my sons, you can take them if I should let any harm come to Benjamin.

ISRAEL: Why would I want more bloodshed

Ruben? This is too much. This is enough. We will find another way to buy food. Find another trade route, and we need to figure out a way to get Simeon. You hear me? But Benjamin is not going anywhere.

RUBEN: Okay, we will do as you wish.

ISRAEL: I need some time. Leave me and make preparation for the people. We will ration what we have and buy ourselves time to figure this out.

The sons leave the room.

ISRAEL: Father what is this? I am trying to do my best by your people and you allow me to lose another son? This is not what you promised me. What happened to the tallest shelve in the family? What happened to being with my family and protecting us? Why would you send us into the pit of the Egyptians with no leverage? Why Father have you felt to judge a old man, brokenhearted, looking for You. Oh, Father surely my death must be near.

FADE to BLACK

NARRATOR: Some months later, after the small rations the brothers were able to obtain from Joseph were gone, they knew they had to have the talk again with their father. With heavy hearts, they return to tell him what he knew would be said. Benjamin would have no choice but to leave his side. There was no food around for miles. He had heard that message for days from the scouts.

ASHER: Father, I know this is hard for you but, Dad if we don't do something we are all going to die of starvation.

ISRAEL: Asher, this cannot be the only way. We can find a way to stretch what we have.

RUBEN: Dad we have already started asking people to fast. We don't have and haven't had food for days. We must prepare for the journey and the last bit of rations was meant to get us there. We have to keep our strength.

DAN: Judah can you talk to him? He wouldn't listen to Ruben.

JUDAH: Father, I heard the Pharaoh say he will not allow us to come back without Benjamin. I only know of one other way to get Simeon back, get food, and leave Benjamin here. What do you want us to do?

ISRAEL: Why did you have to mention him? Why did you have to say that there are twelve and not ten, the number before him?

JUDAH: Ruben didn't know that the mighty Pharaoh would require us to bring him. We wanted to prove we were not spies or liars. We were being truthful, withholding nothing to be found blameless.

GAD: We even spoke about Joseph, to prove we are sincere.

ISRAEL: If anything should happen to Benjamin, I don't know what I would do.

JUDAH: Father we do understand losing Joseph was not easy for you and none of us. We all mourn the death of Joseph, but holding the family back like this won't change what is to come. We need food. We need Benjamin. We need you to be okay with this. I give my word, nothing will happen to him. I will give my life protecting this family. Should anything attempt to happen to Benjamin, I will give my life for his without question.

ISRAEL: I don't want to do this.

Benjamin enters.

BENJAMIN: Dad, let me help. I want to go. It is not fair for all of us to stay here and die if it could be avoided by me going. Please let me go.

ISRAEL: Benjamin, please don't break my heart.

JUDAH: We will watch him. Trust us on that.

ASHER: Ruben promised you the death of both his sons if anything should happen to Benjamin. You think we are not taking this seriously?

GAD: We are all prepared to die for him, if we must die let us die saving and protecting him and our people.

DAN: If we don't go, try, we are dead already.

RUBEN: Dad, this is what we must do.

ISRAEL: Very well, you have all weighed me down. Benjamin, you can go. Judah, you must keep him. Should anything happen to him, I wouldn't be able to bare it. Levi, pray for my strength. Ruben, lead your brothers honorably.

The Lights Fade.

Scene Eighteen

Optional: Video Element - The brothers are back before the Pharaoh. They present Benjamin and he sees them all plead their case of not being spies.

RUBEN: Pharaoh, we have returned with our brother, Benjamin. The eleven brothers are now all here.

JOSEPH: Why did it take you so long to return?

JUDAH: Our father was in mourning. He is very attached to our little brother since his older brother has passed.

JOSEPH: Very well. I believe you are not spies. As an apology for the added inconvenience, I invite you all to dine with me on this evening.

RUBEN: Thank you. We will join you, but must leave soon to return to our father.

JOSEPH: Very well.

NARRATOR: The brothers join Joseph at his home for dinner. At the table is Simeon who awaits his brothers to join him. The brothers see him and embrace him.

NAPHTALI: Brother, how are you?

SIMEON: Well. I wasn't treated like a prisoner. My treatment was incredibly kind.

RUBEN: I am relived to hear it.

ASHER: For more reasons than one, I am too. We know that you are the hot head.

They all joke and sit down. They await for Joseph to join them.

SIMEON: Benjamin, so dad let you finally out the house?

BENJAMIN: Yeah, I am here in the flesh.

Joseph enters and the brothers quiet down.

JOSEPH: Please don't stop on my account.

DAN: Thank you Pharaoh for allowing us to return to you and be here at your table. We were just joking and embracing our brother.

ISSACHAR: Yes, thank you for releasing Simeon and treating him so well.

JOSEPH: Of course. We are not barbarians. We know how to treat guest. He was only a spy if his brothers didn't return. So, tell me, who all sits at this very long table.

JUDAH: I am Judah, here is GAD, DAN, ASHER,

JOSEPH: This young guy, is he

BENJAMIN: I am Benjamin.

JOSEPH: Yes, Benjamin. Thank you for coming. I can see now that you all are a very large family. But I thought you said there was more of you?

ZEBULUN: Yes, our brother Joseph is dead. So he is not around the table.

JOSEPH: Dead?

RUBEN: Yes, it has been nearly twenty-two years. We still speak of him as our brother because he has never left our hearts.

JOSEPH: Got it. I have gifts for you all that I will send home with you.

DAN: We also have brought back a double portion to you, because the last time we came the money we paid was returned back to us.

JOSEPH: I received my money. The money in your sacks must have been from your God.

ASHER: Glad to hear it. Thank you so much for your kindness Pharaoh. We are speechless for your kindness.

JOSEPH: Let's enjoy our meal.

Joseph leans over to Benjamin.

JOSEPH: Can I ask you a question?

BENJAMIN: Yes.

JOSEPH: Come with me.

They both get up and walk towards a different part of the stage, likely a balcony.

JOSEPH: Can you see the stars Benjamin?

The two look out to the stars/sky.

BENJAMIN: Yes, I can. They are vividly bright.

JOSEPH: Can you read them?

BENJAMIN: I can. My father taught me.

JOSEPH: Look at the stars Benjamin, and tell me what do you see.

Benjamin gazes longer at the stars and he is struck with surprise. Joseph reaches out to catch him before he faints, and with a quick shake of the head, Benjamin comes around and embraces him.

JOSEPH: My father taught me how to read the stars also. I knew who you were when you walked in.

BENJAMIN: So it is true. You are my long lost brother. The brother of my mother Rachel?

JOSEPH: It is true.

BENJAMIN: But how did you get all of this? How are you even alive? We thought you were dead.

JOSEPH: I will explain everything to you, but I need to ask you, do you trust me?

Benjamin looks at him for a moment and says.

BENJAMIN: Yes, I trust you.

JOSEPH: There is something I must do and I need you to go with it. There will be nothing that happens to you or our brothers, but I need to know, who they are today. I need to know they are changed. Trust me and help me do this.

BENJAMIN: You have my word.

The two rejoin the table.

Fade.

NARRATOR: The brothers were full and ready to head back home to their families. They each had a sack full of food and gifts from Joseph for their journey home.

JOSEPH: I have spared you all nothing. But now I am insulted.

RUBEN: What is this?

JOSEPH: I gave you all good gifts did I not? I fed you, and allowed you to take up time in my evening. Then you return my hospitality by stealing from me.

ASHER: What are you talking about? We are not thieves?

JOSEPH: I will search your sacks and be the judge of that.

SIMEON: And if we refuse?

JOSEPH: I will believe you all are spies and sentence you accordingly. I am not interested in punishing you all for stealing from me. Just the brother that would dare to steal a cup from my table. The brother who has the cup from my table, will be ordered to remain here with me for the remaining days of his life. The rest of you can leave and go home. Guards! Search their bags!

The guards search the bags of the brothers and find the cup in Benjamin's sack.

JUDAH: Woe, woe, surely there must be a mistake. Benjamin would have never taken a cup from any man's table. This is a mistake or a plot. I am not sure of either, but I cannot return home without my youngest brother.

ASHER: This would pain our father to death and all of us are prepared to bring him home.

JOSEPH: Is that a threat?

GAD: He has already lost a son and thought

he lost Simeon. His spirits were low, this would crush him. This would not be well for our father, but also no one here.

DAN: Pharaoh, surely there has been a mistake or something? May I suggest you work this out.

JUDAH: Pharaoh, I understand it may not make a difference to you who stays behind, but if a life must be stayed surely it should be mine. I gave our father my word I would give my life for my brother's. We love him and his life means the same to all of us. We are all willing to exchange our sons, our lives, and those of whom we love to protect Benjamin. Grant my request.

JOSEPH: Guards, standby. I do not believe this. Surely you were spies. I should have never trusted you. I invited you all to my table, shared my delicacies, and then you betray me by stealing my cup.

JUDAH: I assure you that none of that has happened today. Although you may feel wronged, I assure you, we will not leave this land without our brothers. I gave my father my word.

RUBEN: I gave the life of my sons to be here and protect Benjamin. I would rather die here fighting for him, then to return home and see my sons cut down.

JOSEPH: Do you really think that ten of you could take on the Kingdom of Egypt?

JUDAH: We did more before, for the right cause, we could have taken every king. For our brother, we will cut down anyone who dares stand in our way.

Judah turns to Naphtali and tells him:

JUDAH: Go and number the streets.

Naphtali exits the stage. Joseph motions for the guards to let him go.

Simeon comes out and stands next to Judah.

SIMEON: Pharaoh, it is not our intent to fight, but we will if we are forced.

JOSEPH: Am I to be afraid?

Judah grabs a stone and crushes it with his thigh.

JOSEPH: Impressive. Manasseh.

Manasseh comes out and grabs a similar stone and crushes it in the same manner.

Ruben looks at his brothers.

RUBEN: This boy must be a Hebrew, but how? Who's child is this?

SIMEON: I don't know what is going on here but we are ready to fight and we will.

Naphtali comes back and gives the numbers to Judah in his ear. The brothers line up and keep their stance.

JUDAH: Okay, we are ready. There will be no more talking if you do not release our brother, we will all fight to the death.

JOSEPH: Is that so?

Simeon lets out a loud war cry that shakes the foundations. Joseph believes they are serious and he calls out for more guards.

JOSEPH: More guards! Bring me more guards!

Guards come in to fill the room. The rumbling of their attire can be heard throughout the kingdom. The sound is so loud, that the Pharaoh comes out to have a word with Joseph.

PHARAOH: Joseph, can you explain to me what is happening right now and why is the entire army in my courts?

JOSEPH: I had to do a test to be sure these men were not spies, and have true intentions towards our good will great Pharaoh. I give you my word, I will settle this with no bloodshed.

PHARAOH: Do you know who these boys are? Do you know what even a handful of them can do? I have heard about their God, and their people. They have before leveled kingdoms in days, with just a handful of them, and I am certain I recognize the two out front. We do not need this kind of trouble right now. Whatever you are doing, do it, but do it quickly.

The Pharaoh disappears off the stage.

JOSEPH: I can't do this anymore... Guards lower your spears, brothers, Hebrews no need to arm yourselves. Guards, you may leave and give us a minute. My heart is heavy and also overjoyed.

The guards leave.

JOSEPH: Do you all not recognize me?

Joseph removes his hat, wipes his face, and calls out to Benjamin. Benjamin comes from the back and his brothers swarm around him. After the reunion. They look back at him and Benjamin announces.

BENJAMIN: Don't you guys recognize him?

JOSEPH: I am Joseph, the brother you all sold into slavery.

The brothers are weak with emotion, Benjamin goes up to embrace him, yet again.

JOSEPH: Benjamin, oh how I have missed you. I didn't get to see you grow up, but you look so much like mother.

BENJAMIN: Dad talks about you all the time. I felt like I knew you growing up.

JOSEPH: That means the world.

The other guys rush to Joseph and embraces him. They are over joyed, and yet full of sorrow, shame, and repentance.

ASHER: I am so sorry. We had no idea it was

you.

GAD: That coat blinded my heart and covered my joy of having you as a brother.

DAN: I was jealous of you.

JUDAH: We all were.

DAN: But we thought if you were the one we bowed to, that made you greater than us.

JOSEPH: Do you understand? None of you are to blame for this. This is the Lord's will. What the Lord wanted to do for me—for us was to bless us all. Had I not been sent to Egypt, what provision would there be for the Hebrew Nation now? We may not always understand the Lord's ways, but we trust Him. I never stopped serving Him, thinking about you all. I learned, "What is for you, is for you."

ASHER: You never change. Man we never stopped thinking about you, it nearly killed father to believe you died.

JOSEPH: Died though? Benjamin told me something about that.

JUDAH: Yeah, we kind of told dad, you died.

DAN: We had no choice. We had the blood, the coat, the goat.

GAD: We couldn't tell him you were sold into slavery, that sounded much worst.

RUBEN: But none of that matters now, you are here, alive! Do you know what this means?

JOSEPH: Yeah, It means we need to tell father I am not dead!

Fade.

NARRATOR: The brothers continued to embrace each other and talk about the promising future. Joseph welcomed the Hebrew nation to come and live in the city of Goshen because the famine was not nearly over. Joseph sent them home with plenty of food, and every need they had was met. He also sent a wagon to travel his father Israel back to Egypt.

Scene Nineteen

The sons return home and enter into their father's room. They gather round about him.

JUDAH: We have returned as promised and here stands Benjamin, Simeon you too have seen.

ISRAEL: Thank you Judah. I knew my sons could do this and I am glad you have.

GAD: But there is still news we want to tell you.

ASHER: When we left there were only eleven of us. But now there are again twelve.

ISRAEL: Don't talk silly to me. Joseph is dead.

DAN: No dad, he is not dead. We sold him into slavery, but did not know where he went. We thought to seek him out but couldn't find the Ishmaelites we sold him to. But he is safe, alive, and the second in command under the Pharaoh of Egypt!

ISRAEL: Don't lie to me. How could this be possible? A Hebrew, lording over Egypt?

JUDAH: Father, it is true. We sold our brother because we were jealous of him, but now he has forgiven us.

ASHER: His dreams were true because we all bowed before him and all the kingdoms bow to him. He sent us back with so much more and even a wagon to take you to Goshen!

ISRAEL: Goshen?

RUBEN: The famine is only begun and will get worst. Joseph sent for us to come and dwell in the land of Goshen so we may not die. They have plenty of food and land for us Dad!

BENJAMIN: Dad look out the window. There's the wagon, and here are some of the gifts Joseph gave me. Guess how I knew who he was? The stars. I knew it was him instantly when I read them. I assure you dad, this is not a trick. Your son lives!

ISRAEL: Truly my twelfth son lives. This day my strength has surely been given back to me. Thank you Elohim for hearing the prayers of this family, and returning my son and his brothers to my side.

RUBEN: Dad, you would have been proud to see how we stayed together. How Judah, Naphtali, and Simeon were ready to war the moment Joseph took Benjamin.

ISRAEL: Took him?

BENJAMIN: We planned the cup at dinner. I

didn't know what Joseph would do, but he said he had to test us.

JUDAH: We got the assignment and we would not fail you Baba.

All the sons go to Israel and gives him a hug.

Fade.

Optional: Video Element - The family is traveling through the desert with their families.

NARRATOR: The Hebrew nation all moved to the land of Egypt and resided in the land of Goshen.

Scene Twenty

Israel is in Egypt and lies on his cot. Joseph comes and sits and talks with him. The two have already embraced and now with tear stained faces they speak.

JOSEPH: Father, there is so much I want to tell you but the most important is that I love you. I never forgot what you told me, and I am so glad for all the time you spent with me.

ISRAEL: Oh, how my heart was waxed sore

when you were gone. I nearly died every time I thought of how I didn't get a chance to finish teaching, to telling you...

JOSEPH: Father, everything I needed I received before the Almighty sent me away. Would you have ever sent me away, or let me out of your sight any other way?

ISRAEL: No.

JOSEPH: This was the way the Lord knew it had to be. To preserve us all for the day in which we live. This was already known and spoken to come to past.

ISRAEL: What is for you is for you.

JOSEPH: Yes it is.

Fade.

POET:
A family once broken is now made whole,
What was in part, was only parted for the purpose of Yah.
Every step you take, each move you make, points to a foundation,
Everything will work to the good of those who love and are called for the Lord's grand plan.

What is for you, is for you.

Song/Dance transition _____

NARRATOR: Joseph and Israel spent many years together before Israel died. His vision began to fade, but the power had not left his body. Before he took his last breath...

ISRAEL: Joseph, come closer son. My days have been made full because I have had the chance to see you, to know your sons, and see you with your brothers. Oh, how great I feel. I'm at peace.

JOSEPH: Father it seems so short still.

ISRAEL: What's for me—

JOSEPH: I know, is for you.

ISRAEL: I need you to do me a favor, and give me your word.

JOSEPH: Whatever you ask, it is done.

ISRAEL: I want for, when I pass, for you to bury me in the land of our fathers. Don't allow my body to rest in Egypt, and also, don't allow your body to rest here either. Please bury me—

JOSEPH: I got it dad. I will bury you, and when I pass, I too will be buried in the land of my forefathers.

JOSEPH: Dad, can you do me one more favor?

ISRAEL: What is it son?

JOSEPH: Bless my sons. Sons, come here.

Manasseh and Ephraim entered into the room and stood next to their grandfather.

ISRAEL: Oh, my soul is so full of joy. I dreamed of only meeting you, and now to see your sons in my old age. To see them grow for these years. I don't know what to say… Come here grandsons.

Israel embraces them and lays his hand on them.

ISRAEL: Grandsons, it blesses my soul to have met you both, and I want to bless you both.

Israel places his hands on the sons.

JOSEPH: Father, you have your right hand on the wrong son. Manasseh is the oldest, not Ephraim.

ISRAEL: I know. I don't see by sight, but by what the Lord is showing me. Both of your sons are blessed, but Ephraim will have a larger kingdom. What is for you is for you. Father bless all of my sons. Bless my grandchildren to have the kingdom, the gifts, the influence, the power they need to fulfill your will in their lives. Thank you for blessing me to give a blessing to each of my sons, and a legacy that goes beyond physical wealth, but to the spiritual.

ISRAEL: As you continue to raise nations even today from their loins, announce in their hearts who they are. Help them to remember their journey. Bless them to know, we walk by faith, by the spirit, and not by sight so that we can have confidence and trust you in all seasons. Shalom, peace and blessings be upon us all.

Fade Out.

Close:

Suggested Last Words from K. Lee:

Video Element - Whatever is for you is for you. No matter what people say about what should be your inheritance, what you deserve, or what you should have, it is not their choice. It should only matter what the Almighty has said about you. If He calls you blessed, what does it matter what people say?

If He blesses you with a little or big house, why does it matter? What is yours is yours, and no one can take it from you. Joseph's brothers thought that by selling him, they would stop his blessing and his promise, but they only helped him to fulfill his purpose. Don't be angry with the people, the choices that appear to be to your harm. Because the Bible says that all things work for the good of those who love the Lord, and are called according to His purpose!

Be encouraged. No matter where you are today, know that Yahweh has a plan for your life. What's for you is for you. May the Elohim who has created the heavens and earth bless and keep you in Yashua's Name, so be it!

Last Words: This play was written by author K Lee. Directed by: "Director," Music by: "Music Director," and performed by this amazing cast! Please welcome back to the stage our incredible cast and crew.

All cast and crew are on stage and take a bow.

About The Author

Growing up, Dr. Krystal Lee, known as Author K. Lee, has always been adventurous in writing, production, business, and being a die-hard entrepreneur. She puts her heart into every project and operates in excellence because that is the standard. She completes every project as if unto Yashua (aka Jesus), and so she regrets nothing.

K. Lee is a strong believer in prayer and believes the Truth sets anyone free. She is grateful that the Almighty has come into her life. He has removed her from a path of self-destruction and set her on a path to keep her heart, mind, and desire set on helping others. As a kid, she wanted to be caviler, not wear her heart on her sleeves, and not cry when she saw others cry. This, however, was not the way the Lord made her.

The Lord called her to have a heart that cares for others. Sympathizes with the afflicted, seeks justice, and helps the needy. K. Lee is passionate about projects that build up people, remove oppression, pain, and deliver hope. Her ambitions as a child were to express her thoughts and those of the silent in music, dance, theater, but especially in writing.

Dr. Krystal Lee has written several books both fiction and non-fiction that she desires to publish during her lifetime. In addition to writing books, K. Lee is passionate about video and media production. She started writing music, then transition to screenplays and theater. K. Lee is a talented singer and actress who prefers to be behind the scenes; she loves to tell a good story.

In addition to her creative talents, she is an entrepreneur owning several businesses. She has established Krystal Lee Enterprises, KLE Services, BWC, Your Legacy Moment for preserving your story, and developing many more companies and concepts. She is also the President of TUG Outreach, a non-profit organization that helps youth and adults by creating programs and offering services to benefit the broader community.

Dr. Krystal Lee is equally passionate about ministry as she is about commerce, entertainment, and writing. She enjoys teaching and speaking on subjects relative to her life experience and anointed ability. She is an ordained Chaplain and Minister, with International accreditation, and she is in training to walk in her calling of being an Apostle. She believes Adonia (The Lord) has a calling on her life to be a mouthpiece for the Lord to those she is sent. She is prepared to follow His voice and travel to where He sends her without the slightest hesitation. Most of her ministry is online and published on social channels like Instagram, Facebook, Youtube, TikTok, LinkedIn, and TUG Network; more outlets are being added.

K. Lee hates religion, spreading faith through fear, and believes in the value of people, no matter their current condition. No one is beyond the healing hand of YHWH if they want help. Help can be offered, but it must always be accepted, which requires choice.

Yashua (aka Jesus) is her Lord and savior, and she looks forward to His coming. The days we live in remind her that the second coming is growing near. She believes and is passionate about helping all who have an ear to hear, hear the Good News.

AuthorKLee.com Creator of *WAE Process*

SCAN ME

Call or Text:
770-240-0089 Press Extension 1
Web: KLEpub.com
Email Services@klepub.com

It's time to start and finish   YOUR Story!

KLE Publishing specializes in helping people become authors. In as little as 15 to 90 days, we can help you develop your books and e-books and publish to 39,000 outlets! We also offer audiobook services.

Write, Edit, Format, Publish
We can help from
Start to Finish.

Explore and learn more about published authors affiliated with KLE.

KLEPub.com

www.ingramcontent.com/pod-product-compliance
Lightning Source LLC
Chambersburg PA
CBHW072013110526
44592CB00012B/1288